A Correspondence Workbook

A Ashley

OXFORD UNIVERSITY PRESS

Oxford University Press
Walton Street, Oxford OX2 6DP

Oxford New York
Athens Auckland Bangkok Bombay
Calcutta Cape Town Dar es Salaam Delhi
Florence Hong Kong Istanbul Karachi
Kuala Lumpur Madras Madrid Melbourne
Mexico City Nairobi Paris Singapore
Taipei Tokyo Toronto

and associated companies in
Berlin Ibadan

Oxford and *Oxford English*
are trade marks of Oxford University Press

ISBN 0 19 457207 2

Typeset by Pentacor PLC
Printed in Hong Kong

Contents

Structure and presentation 1

1.a Read the following statements and decide which are true T and which are false F.

1 If a letter begins with the receiver's name, e.g. *Dear Mr Ross*, it will close with *Yours faithfully*. ☐
2 The abbreviation *c.c.* stands for 'correct carbons'. ☐
3 If you were writing a letter to Mr Peter Smith, you would open with *Dear Mr Peter Smith.* ☐
4 The head of a company in the UK is known as 'The President'. ☐
5 In the USA, it is correct to open a letter with the salutation *Gentlemen*. ☐
6 The abbreviation *enc* or *encl* means there are enclosures with the letter. ☐
7 If you were writing to a Knight whose name was Sir Roger Dumont, you would open the letter *Dear Sir Dumont*. ☐
8 In the UK, the abbreviated date 2.6.95 on a letter means 6 February 1995. ☐
9 If a secretary signs her name on a letter and her signature is followed by *p.p.* (per pro) *Daniel Harris*, it means she is signing on behalf of Daniel Harris. ☐
10 A Managing Director in the UK is known as Chief Executive in the USA. ☐
11 The term *PLC* after a company's name, e.g. *Hathaway PLC*, stands for 'Public Limited Corporation'. ☐
12 The abbreviation for the term 'limited liability' in the UK, is *ltd*. ☐
13 If you did not know whether a female correspondent was married or not, it would be correct to use the term *Ms*, e.g. *Ms Tessa Groves*, instead of *Miss* or *Mrs*. ☐
14 The following is an example of a blocked style: ☐

Peter Voss
Oberlweinfeldweg 33
5207 Therwil
Switzerland

15 The above address is an example of 'open punctuation'. ☐
16 The abbreviation in addressing a doctor, e.g. *Doctor James Spock*, would be *Dt. Spock*. ☐
17 Rather than use the UK close of *Yours sincerely/faithfully*, Americans often choose *Yours truly*. ☐
18 The abbreviation for 'company' is *Co*. ☐

1.b   Put the verbs in brackets into either the present simple, (e.g. *he works*), or the present continuous, (e.g. *he is working*).

1   ICI (be) a large multinational company that (export) to countries all over the world.
2   The Managing Director (have) a meeting at the moment, but I will ask him to call you back.
3   Although the economic climate (improve) slowly, a lot of smaller companies (find) trading conditions difficult at the moment.
4   Office workers in the UK normally (start) at 9 a.m. and (go) home at 5 p.m.
5   At the moment the Sales Director is on a two-week tour of Europe, where he (meet) suppliers and (do) some market research.
6   We now (need) to expand, so we (negotiate) the lease of larger offices outside London.
7   I (write) to you to enquire about the possibility of setting up an agency in Spain for your products.
8   I (try) to get in touch with Mr Peters, but I (not/have) much luck. He still (have) the same phone number?

1.c   Put the following names and addresses in order.

Example
Search Studios Ltd./Leeds/LS4 8QM/Mr L. Scott/150 Royal Avenue

Mr L. Scott
Search Studios Ltd.
150 Royal Avenue
Leeds LS4 8QM

1   Warwick House/Soundsonic Ltd./London/Warwick Street/SE23 1JF
2   Piazza Leonardo da Vinci 254/The Chief Accountant/I-20133/D. Fregoni/Fregoni S.p.A./Milano
3   Bente Spedition GmbH/Mr Heinz Bente/D-6000 Frankfurt 1/Feldbergstr. 30/The Chairman
4   Sportique et cie./201 rue Sambin/The Sales Manager/F-21000 Dijon
5   Intercom/E-41006 Sevilla/351 Avda. Luis de Morales/The Accountant/Mrs S. Moreno
6   Miss Maria Nikolakaki/85100 Rhodes, Nikitara 541/Greece
7   Excel Heights 501/Edogawa-ku 139/7–3–8 Nakakasai/Japan/Tokyo/Mrs Junko Shiratori
8   301 Leighton Road/VHF Vehicles Ltd./London NW5 2QE/The Transport Director/Kentish Town

1.d Using either the present simple or present continuous tenses, complete the letter with the appropriate verb from the list below.

build   look   offer   start   write
know   note   provide   supply

HALL & CO. LTD
Builders' Merchants

Dear Sir/Madam,

We (1)_____ that you have made a planning application and (2)_____ an extension to your property soon, and I (3)_____ to inform you of the services which we, as your local Builders' Merchant, (4)_____ for our customers.

Our range of products (5)_____ at the foundations with sand, cement, and bricks, and we also (6)_____ a full range of timber and plasterboard products.

In addition to this, but only for the next two weeks, we (7)_____ a free estimating service, so that you (8)_____ exactly how much the materials will cost.

We (9)_____ forward to hearing from you.

Yours faithfully,

Hall and Co. Ltd

1.e   Complete the following letter of enquiry with the correct prepositions.

Velo Sport AG
Karlstr. 45
0–5230 Sömmerda

The Sales Director   15 February 19 —
UK Cycles Ltd
Borough House
Borough Road
Cleveland TS8 3BA

Dear Sir,

We read your advertisement (1)_____, racing cycles
(2)_____ the current edition (3)_____ *Cyclists*
and are interested (4)_____ your products, particularly
touring bikes.

We are a large retail company, (5)_____ cycle shops
throughout Germany and would like your catalogue and a price-
list, quoting c.i.f. Berlin prices.

Please let us know your terms (6)_____ trade, including
quantity discounts, delivery dates, and any credit facilities your
are prepared to offer (7)_____ large orders.

We look forward (8)_____ hearing (9)_____
you soon.

Yours faithfully,

Karl Janssen

Karl Janssen
Managing Director

1.f   Write a letter of reply from Robert Morris, Sales Director of UK Cycles, to Karl Janssen.

- Thank him for his letter, quoting the date.
- Give him the following information:
  Discounts – quantity discounts on orders over £10,000.
  Delivery time – usually three months after receipt of order.
  Credit – facilities only after trading for at least one year with the company.
- Thank him for his interest in your company, and close the letter in the appropriate manner.

Content and Style

2

2.a Read this letter from a computer company to a company trainer, and fill in the blanks with the correct verb taken from the list below.

leave	will travel	will be staying	will have had
suit	will be met	will be visiting	will have returned
arrive	will need		
	will not be able		

Dear Mr Jackson,

Re: Nicosia Computer Training Course

Thank you for your letter of 18 May giving us the dates of your visit. I am writing to inform you of the arrangements we have made on your behalf.

You (1)_____ at Larnaca airport by the company driver, and (2)_____ at the Amathus Beach Hotel for the first night. When you (3)_____ Larnaca, you (4)_____ up to Nicosia and spend four days at the training centre. Most of the trainee operators (5)_____ some experience of the new program by the time you (6)_____, but they (7)_____ some instruction on the more complex areas of the system.

Unfortunately, Mr Charalambides (8)_____ to meet you on Thursday 15 June, as you requested, because he (9)_____ our subsidiary in Spain. However, he (10)_____ by the following Monday, 19 June, so I have arranged for him to see you at 2.30 p.m.

Please let me know if these arrangements (11)_____ you. I look forward to hearing from you.

Yours sincerely,

Elena Theodorou

Elena Theodorou
Training Manager

2.b Put the phrases below in the correct order to form a letter requesting information.

Dear Sir/Madam,

☐ which was held last June,

☐ and may be interested in retailing them through our outlets in Germany.

☐ We saw a large selection of your products at the Frankfurt Fair,

☐ Could you send us your latest catalogue and price-list,

☐ We are particularly interested in your industrial ware,

☐ quoting c.i.f. terms to Hamburg.

☐ including overalls, boots, helmets, gloves, and fire-proof jackets.

☐ We look forward to hearing from you soon.

☐ We can assure you that if your prices and discounts are competitive,

☐ Yours faithfully,

☐ Chief Buyer

☐ we will place regular large orders.

☐ T. Hamacher

2.c Rewrite the following request for payment in a more polite form.

Dear Sir,

Your have owed us £567.00 since February, which means you haven't paid us for three months.

We wrote to you twice and amazingly you didn't bother answering us, yet you've been a customer for years. Anyway, we're not going on like this, so if you don't tell us why you haven't paid, or send the money you owe us in ten days, we'll sue you. After all, we've got bills from our own suppliers, and besides we explained our rules for giving credit, i.e. payment on final dates, some time ago.

R. Lancaster

Yours, etc.

R. Lancaster

2.d The following is the reply to the letter in Exercise 2.c. It was received by R. Lancaster's secretary. Write a memo from the secretary to her boss, telling him about the reply, and summarizing its contents.

Dear Sir,

I am writing to you in reply to your letter dated 9 May, which we received on 10 May, in which you reminded us of our outstanding balance, which now amounts to the sum total of £567.00.

I should like to offer my humblest apologies for our failure either to settle the account, or to reply to your two previous communications. However, I feel that I must explain the cause of this oversight. We have been the unfortunate victims of a tragedy. Two months ago, our premises were almost completely destroyed by fire. Although I am happy to report that we sustained no casualties, all our accounts records, stock, orders ready for despatch and so on, were consumed by the flames.

Now, at last, our fortunes are beginning to rise again, and our insurance company will shortly be releasing funds to facilitate our recovery. Let me assure you that you will be remunerated in full as soon as possible. In the interim, I would be grateful if you would accept a small sum towards the settlement of our account, with my personal promise that the remaining amount will be forwarded to you as soon as it becomes available.

Please find enclosed a cheque for the sum of £55.00, and once again, I beg you to accept my deepest apologies for any inconvenience caused.

Yours faithfully,

T. D. Games

T. D. Games

2.e   Follow the instructions in this memo, and write a letter, setting it out in the spaces provided on the opposite page.

Sarah Barnard is Managing Director of Barnard Press Ltd., 183–7 Copwood Road, North Finchley, London N12 9PR, and Rosalind Wood is her secretary.

MEMO

To: Rosalind   **Date:** 1 March 19 —
From: Sarah

Please type a reply to Claudio Bini of International Books.

Address: Via Santovetti 117/9, 00045 Grottaferratta, Rome, Italy.

Use reference RW/SB

His letter dated 15 Feb

He asked about story-books in English and Italian for intermediate students. Tell him they're out of stock at the moment, but we'll be publishing a new list of them this summer. Send him details of the new list, and a current catalogue of present stock.

Thanks.

R. Wood

Enquiries

3

3.a   Complete this letter of enquiry. Decide whether to use *a*, *the*, or no article at all, in the blank spaces.

Thank you for your letter giving us (1)_____ details of (2)_____ products we enquired about.

(3)_____ main item we are interested in is (4)_____ kitchen unit listed in (5)_____ catalogue under (6)_____ heading CM214. As we are building (7)_____ large block of apartments, we think (8)_____ unit like (9)_____ one listed, might be (10)_____ best installation for our purposes.

Please let us know what your terms of (11)_____ trade are. Could you also tell us if you are able to offer (12)_____ trade and (13)_____ quantity discounts on (14)_____ price for (15)_____ large order? We would also be grateful for (16)_____ samples of all materials used in (17)_____ manufacture of your units.

I am including (18)_____ plan of our apartments, and (19)_____ dimensions we would need.

3.b   Match these words from Exercise 3.a with their definitions.

a	catalogue	1	details of conditions of sale
b	trade discount	2	price reduction to a company in the same business
c	order	3	a small amount of a product offered free to a potential customer
d	quantity discount	4	book giving details of items for sale
e	sample	5	request from a customer to supply goods
f	terms of trade	6	price reduction for a large order

3.c Rewrite the following questions in a less direct form, beginning with the words given.

Examples
What are your terms of trade?
Please let us know *what your terms of trade are*.

Are you able to offer us trade and quantity discounts on large orders?
Could you also tell us *if you are able to offer trade and quantity discounts on large orders*.

1 Could you send me a copy of your latest brochure?

   I would be grateful _____

2 How much discount will you give on orders of 5,000 units?

   Could you please tell us _____

3 When can we expect to receive the cheque?

   I am writing to enquire _____

4 Would you like us to arrange an appointment with one of our representatives?

   Please let us know _____

5 Has Mr Crane returned from the Menswear Exhibition yet?

   Do you happen to know _____

6 Does your company export to South Korea?

   Could you tell us _____

3.d Make words from the jumbled letters and match them with the definitions in the sentences below.

a UEAGTOCLA   c METIESAT   e RENTED   g ETSMCOUR
b LAOEEHSLWR   d WOSORHOM   f IDISYUSRAB h OSSUTCREPP

1 A company or organization that is part of a larger one.
2 A person who buys items from a shop or company.
3 A room where companies demonstrate their products.
4 A kind of magazine giving details of the items a company sells.
5 A prediction of how much an item or service is likely to cost.
6 A written quotation for a large job such as building a factory.
7 A kind of magazine giving details about a school, college, or university.
8 A company or person that buys and sells items only in bulk.

3.e   John Phillips is telling his secretary what to write when she types out the day's letters. Change his instructions into an acceptable form for business correspondence.

Example
J.P. Ask them for a cash discount.
Sec *Could you offer us a cash discount?*

1   Ask for more information about prices.

_____

2   We're out of stock at the moment. Ask them to try again in two weeks.

_____

3   Say that we want these items delivered in three months.

_____

4   Ask them to send us a catalogue and price-list.

_____

5   Find out what their terms of trade are.

_____

6   Tell them to get in touch with us if they can't deliver the goods before Friday.

_____

7   Say that we'd like them to send someone here to give an estimate.

_____

8   Find out if we can get twenty units on approval.

_____

3.f Complete the following letter of enquiry with the correct prepositions.

Avda. San Antonio 501
80260 Bellaterra
Barcelona

Admissions Dept.   12 October 19 —
The International College
145–8 Regents Road
Falmer
Brighton BN1 9QN

Dear Sir/Madam,

I am a Spanish student (1)_____ the University
(2)_____ Barcelona doing a Master's Course
(3)_____ Business Studies, and I intend to spend six
months (4)_____ England, (5)_____ January next
year, preparing (6)_____ the Cambridge First
Certificate.

Your college was recommended (7)_____ me
(8)_____ a fellow student and I would like details
(9)_____ the First Certificate course, including fees and
dates. Could you also let me know if you can provide
accommodation (10)_____ me (11)_____ Brighton
(12)_____ an English family.

Thank you for your attention, and I look forward to hearing
from you soon.

Yours faithfully,

Maria Ortega
Maria Ortega

3.g You are Carol Ross, and you are organizing a business trip to Frankfurt for yourself and two colleagues. Write to a travel agency for information, using the following guide.

- Say what you are planning to do.
- Ask the travel agency to send details of flights and hotel tariffs for the month of March. Find out if it is necessary to pay a deposit on the trip.
- Tell them that you would also like to hire a car for two days during your stay, and ask them to send you details.
- Thank them, mentioning that you need a prompt reply.

3.h   Read this reply to a letter of enquiry. Underline the words in the letter which correspond to the words and phrases below.

1 selling through shops	3 set up	5 be sorry	7 range
2 reply	4 conditions	6 up-to-date	8 extremely

GLASTON POTTERIES Ltd

Clayfield, Burnley BB10 1RQ
Tel: 0315 46125   Telex: 8801773   Fax: 0315 63182

Mr J. F. Morreau   2 July 19 —
1150 boulevard Calbert
F–54015 Nancy Cedex

Dear Mr Morreau,

Thank you for your enquiry of 28 June in which you expressed an interest in retailing a selection of our products in your shops in France.

Please find enclosed our current brochure and price list.

In response to your request for a 20% trade discount, we regret that we cannot offer more than 15%. However, we do give a 5% quantity discount on orders over £10,000. We are sure that you will agree that these terms are highly competitive.

We are confident that we can deliver within two months as you require, but wish to emphasize that payment will have to be by sight draft until we have established a business relationship.

Thank you for your interest and we hope to hear from you soon.

Yours sincerely.

J. Merton

J. Merton
Sales Manager

Enc.

3.i   Write the letter of enquiry which preceded the reply in Exercise 3.h. You are J. F. Morreau, and you have just seen an advertisement for Glaston Potteries Willow Pattern dinner sets in the May edition of *International Homes*.

Replies and quotations

4

4.a
4.a Read the following reply to a letter of enquiry. Mr Fest refers to specific questions asked by Mr Whang. Which of the items below did he request information about?

1 how soon the goods can be delivered
2 details of prices
3 where the goods can be purchased
4 after-sales service
5 how the goods will be transported
6 terms of payment
7 quantity discounts
8 cash discounts
9 details of the range of goods available
10 which bank will handle the transaction
11 guarantees

Dear Mr Whang,

Thank you for your enquiry of 16 August concerning our equipment, which you saw at the International Farm Machinery Fair in Bonn.

In answer to the specific questions in your letter, first let me say we are willing to consider substantial discount on orders over 200,000 DM.

All our machinery is guaranteed for three years against normal use, and we have several agencies in your country with home-trained mechanics to service all our products.

With regard to the terms of payment, which you mentioned, we would consider payment by 30-day bill of exchange, documents against acceptance, provided you could offer two referees.

We can fulfil orders within three months, unless there are special specifications, which may take a little longer, and you can buy equipment from us, or through our agents in your country.

We are enclosing our current catalogue and price-list quoting c.i.f. Bangkok prices, which you requested, and we think you will find the earth-moving equipment on pp 101–115 particularly interesting for the work you have in mind. If you require any further information, please contact us and we will be pleased to supply it.

Yours sincerely,

Gustav Fest

Gustav Fest
Sales Director

4.b   Here are some of the questions Mr Whang asked. Rewrite them in reported speech.

Example
Do you offer discount on large orders?
He asked if *they offered discounts on large orders*.

1 How soon can the goods be delivered?

He asked _____

2 Can you send me details of your prices?

He asked for _____

3 Where can the goods be purchased?

He wanted to know _____

4 Is there an after-sales service?

He asked _____

5 How long are the goods guaranteed for?

He asked _____

6 What are your terms of payment?

He wanted to know _____

7 Do you give quantity discounts, and how much are they?

He asked _____

8 Can you send me details of the range of goods available?

He wondered _____

4.c Read the following letter of reply and choose the best words from the options in brackets.

Dear Mr Osterheld,

We were very pleased to receive your [1](*correspondence, enquiry, mail*) of 14 October 19 —, asking about our leather and sheepskin [2](*range, cloths, products*) and terms of [3](*dealing, trade, conditions*).

First let me say that our [4](*label, mark patent*) is internationally famous because of the quality of our garments, and we are convinced they will sell very well through your [5](*outlets, factories, warehouses*). We think you will agree with us when you look through the enclosed [6](*manual, catalogue, leaflet*) and examine the [7](*specimens, examples, samples*) we are forwarding separately.

You will see from the price-list that we take care of all freight and insurance costs, so the prices are quoted on a(n) [8](*c.i.f., ex-works, f.o.b.*) basis. We will also allow [9](*trade, cash, quantity*) discounts for orders over $10,000, and with the usual trade references, we can arrange for payment by 60-day [10](*bill, letter, draft*) of exchange.

Thank you once again for your enquiry, and we are sure you will be impressed by the [11](*vast, huge, wide*) selection of our garments. Meanwhile, if there are any further details you need, please contact us.

Yours sincerely,

Ellena Onate

Ellena Onate
Sales Director

4.d   Put the verbs in brackets into the gerund, (e.g. *doing*) or infinitive, (e.g. *to do*) in the following letter.

Example
We thought of (go) into this market.
We thought of going into this market.

1   After (discuss) the terms of your offer, I regret (say) our board has decided (delay) its decision.
2   You probably remember us (ask) for trade and quantity discounts.
3   Unfortunately, the discounts offered would not be sufficient (make) half the profits we had calculated.
4   I have pleasure in (enclose) your estimate.
5   We would be interested in (retail) a selection of your products, and look forward to (receive) your samples.
6   After successfully (promote) this product in France, we now plan (launch) it onto the Italian market.

4.e   Complete this letter of enquiry with the correct prepositions.

GDM Ltd

516 Gipsey Rd Headington Oxford OX3 6BP UK

The Chairman
Busch AG
Leopoldstr. 501
D–8000 München 3   10 June 19 —

Dear Sir,

We were impressed (1)_____ your display (2)_____ office
furniture (3)_____ the Expoquip trade fair held (4)_____
Madrid (5)_____ January.

We are a group (6)_____ retailers specializing (7)_____ the
sale (8)_____ top–quality non-electronic office equipment, and we are
seeking a supplier (9)_____ our stores.

Could you send us your latest catalogue and price-list, details
(10)_____ materials used (11)_____ your products, and
information regarding credit terms and discounts?

We look forward (12)_____ receiving your reply.

Yours faithfully,

Anne Croft

Anne Croft (Miss)
Sales Director

4.f Now read this memo from Gerd Busch, of Busch AG to his secretary. Use the information to write a letter of reply to Anne Croft from the secretary, on Mr Busch's behalf.

MEMO

To: Birgit Lange   **Date:** 14 June 19 —

From: G. Busch

Please reply to this letter. Send Miss Croft a catalogue and price-list and quote her c.i.f. prices to London.

Mention also the following:

    2-year guarantee on all our products

    Highest-quality materials used

    No credit terms (our prices highly competitive due to small profit margins)

    Cash discount of 3 per cent offered

Do encourage her to contact us again.

Thanks.

Orders

5

5.a Use the words below to complete this extract from a covering letter that has been sent with an order.

depot   consignment   crates
wrapped   settle   hand over
transaction   packed
delivery   alternative

Would you please make sure that the (1)_____
of fabrics is (2)_____ carefully in tissue paper,
and (3)_____ securely in
(4)_____ and sent to our main goods
(5)_____ at the above address in Milan.

If the items listed are not available, please do not send
(6)_____ materials or colours. If there are any
problems with (7)_____, could you let us know
immediately.

We will (8)_____ your draft for 25,000 DM, at
our bank as soon as they (9)_____ the shipping
documents.

If this (10)_____ is successful, we will place
larger orders in the future.

5.b Match up the phrases in **A** with the phrases in **B** to make complete sentences, and put the verbs into the first conditional.

Example
If there (be) any delay . . .   . . . we (inform) you at once.
If there is any delay, we will inform you at once.

A

1 Unless the consignment (arrive) by the end of next week, . . .
2 We (be able) to give you a discount . . .
3 Unless the items (be/wrap) with extreme care . . .
4 If the colours we specified (be) not in stock, . . .
5 We (send) the consignment by road . . .
6 If this transaction (be) successful, . . .

B

a . . . if you (order) more than 20,000 units.
b . . . we (place) further orders with you.
c . . . we (accept) an alternative.
d . . . we (have to) cancel the order.
e . . . many of them (get) broken.
f . . . if the railways (be) still on strike.

5.c Complete each unfinished sentence in the exercise below, so that it means the same as the one before it.

1 If we don't hear from you, we'll assume there are no problems.

   Unless we _____

2 We can't give you a fifteen per cent discount because your order isn't large enough.

   If your order _____

3 On receipt of your order, we'll despatch the goods immediately.

   As soon as we _____

4 We can only process your order if we receive the necessary documents within fourteen days.

   Provided that we _____

5 The colour you require may be out of stock. Would you accept an alternative?

   If we _____ ?

6 We cannot accept your order without a letter of credit.

   Unless you _____

5.d   The following verbs can all be used with the noun *order*. Choose the best verb to complete the sentences, using each one only once, in the correct form.

confirm   refuse   deliver   ship
place   make up   cancel   despatch

1   We should like to _____ an order with you for 5,000 units.

2   As we are unable to supply the quantity you requested, it would be quite

    understandable for you to _____ your order.

3   We are confident that we will be able to _____ the order to you
    next week.

4   You will be pleased to know that your order K451 has already been

    _____ from our depot.

5   Please _____ your order in writing, so we can inform our
    distribution depot.

6   Your order was _____ yesterday on the SS Oxford.

7   Unfortunately, we shall have to _____ your order unless payment
    is settled in cash.

8   I would like to reassure you that your order will be _____ in our
    depot by staff who have experience in handling these delicate materials.

5.e   Read this extract from a letter apologizing for a delayed delivery, and choose the
best words from the options in brackets.

Further to our telephone conversation, I am writing to you
[1](*affecting, concerning, changing*) your order, No. SX1940,
which was [2](*sold, made, placed*) with us on 10 January.

Once again, I must [3](*regret, apologize, speak*) to you for our
delay in processing the order. This was due to a [4](*shortage,
fault, problem*) of office staff. However, since I spoke to you
last week, we have [5](*dismissed, promoted, taken on*) four new
employees at our depot, and I am pleased to be able to tell
you that your order is now ready for despatch. It will [6](*arrive,
delivery, reach*) you in approximately fourteen days' time.

As always, special [7](*care, attention, caution*) has been taken to
ensure that your [8](*load, crates, consignment*) of goods has
been packed [9](*meeting, according, serving*) to your
requirements. Each item will be individually wrapped to
[10](*prevent, cause, stop*) damage.

5.f   Read the following memo from a buying manager to a secretary.

MEMORANDUM

To: Sabine Muss

From: D. Faust (Buying Manager)

Date: 5 May 19 —

Please place an order with D. Causio of Satex for the
items I've indicated on the catalogue attached. Remind
him in the accompanying letter that the terms we agreed
on were payment by banker's draft, and delivery within
six weeks.

Thank you.

Now look at the sales catalogue Mr Faust mentioned in his memo.

SATEX S.p.A.
Spring catalogue

ITEM		CATALOGUE NO.	PRICE (DM per item)	
Shirts				
Plain	white	S298	30	*50*
	blue	S288	30	*50*
Striped	white/blue	S301	35	
	white/grey	S302	35	
	white/green	S303	35	
Pullovers (V-neck)				
Plain	red	P112	40	*20*
	blue	P155	40	*20*
	black	P196	40	
Patterned	blue	P305	52	
	black	P306	52	

Now, use the information from the memo and the catalogue to complete the order form.

SATEX S.p.A.
Via di Pietra Papa 00146 Roma

ORDER FORM

Date: 5 May 19 —

Name of company: Reiner GmbH

Order No: W6164

Telephone: 05 41/7/98 25 21

Fax: 05 41/3 82 21

Telex: 2918176

Address for delivery: Wessumerstrasse 215–18, D–4500 Osnabrück

Authorized: _____ (D. Faust)

Quantity	Item description	Cat No.	Price c.i.f.	Total

Amount due: _____

Terms of payment: _____

Requested delivery date: _____

5.g   Write a covering letter with this order from Sabine Muss on behalf of D. Faust.

- Thank Satex for their letter of 1 May, catalogue, and price-list.
- Tell them you have enclosed the above order, and that you expect delivery within six weeks. You will pay by banker's draft when you receive the shipping documents.
- Explain that if items are not available they should not send substitutes.
- Tell them that if there are any problems with delivery, they must let you know at once.
- Close by saying you look forward to receiving acknowledgement of your order.

5.h Write a covering letter from Anne Lenoir for an order according to the instructions in the memo below.

YACHT INTERNATIONALE

12 BVD SALVADOR   F–13006 MARSEILLE

MEMO

To: Anne Lenoir   *Date:* 25 September 19 —

From: Jacques Delmas

Please write a covering letter to accompany Order R497. Despatch details as follows:

Name of supplier: Mr H. Kjaer (Sales Director)
Address: Dansk Industries, Kongens Nytorv 1, DK–1050 København K.
Consignment: navigational instruments

Please remind Dansk to pack the goods individually in 8 crates, numbered, with our logo. Tell them to send the instruments air freight, c.i.f. Marseille, to reach us no later than 18 May.

Their invoice should show all individual costs and the 12% trade and 3% quantity discounts we agreed on. Remind them to send this with the insurance certificate, and Air Waybill to The Bank of Marseille, 153–6 avenue Charles de Gaulle, F–12019, Marseille, where we will hand over our sight draft.

Thank you.

Payment

6

6.a Put *who*, *that*, *which*, or preposition + *which* in the following sentences, where necessary.

1 Thank you for your letter _____ you enquired about our products.

2 Your statement of account, _____ we received yesterday, appears

to have a number of errors _____ refer to items we did not order.

3 I would like to speak to Mr Newland, _____ phoned me earlier,

concerning our account, _____ he says has not been cleared.

4 The cheque _____ you sent us has now been cleared.

5 Would you please clear your balance _____ has been
outstanding since February.

6 You need to contact the person _____ deals with foreign
transactions.

6.b Look at these two sentences:

We received your Giro slip today informing *us that you had paid £126.00 into your
account.*
I rang the manager to inform *him that I had paid off the outstanding balance.*

In which sentence does the verb mean 'which informed'?
In which sentence does the verb mean 'in order to inform'?

Now complete the following sentences using the verbs either as participles (e.g.
working), or infinitives (e.g. *to work*).

1 Mrs Jackson has gone to the Post office (cash) _____ a postal
order.

2 They sent us an invoice (give) _____ details of all the goods that
had been ordered.

3 Their letter, (explain) _____ why they had not paid promptly,
arrived a few days later.

4   I am writing to you (ask) _____ why the outstanding balance on
    your account has still not been paid.

5   I have written to the insurers (find out) _____ when they expect to
    settle the claim.

6   Although I am reluctant to take legal action (recover) _____ the
    amount, you leave me no alternative.

7   In our company we normally use letters of credit (settle) _____
    transactions overseas.

6.c   Find the missing words in the wordbox below.

ACROSS

1   A _____ note is a form of an IOU.
2   If you want your money back, ask for a _____ .
3   An _____ records goods or services that have been sold.
4   An International Money _____ can be bought at the bank to settle
    accounts abroad.
5   Large purchases such as cars can be paid for by Bank _____ .
6   After three requests for payment you might receive a final _____ .
7   A postal cheque system, run by the post office, is called _____ .

DOWN

8   A _____ invoice may be used when the customer has to pay in advance.
    (2 words, 3–4)
9   Banks will _____ money from one account to another by order.

6.d   Match each sentence written in formal English (i.e. the appropriate language for letter-writing), to its nearest informal equivalent.

Example
We expect to receive a remittance from you in seven days.
a   We want you to get in touch with us in a week.
b   We would like you to pay your debt in the next week.
c   We want you to send our account details next week.

1   We should like another month to settle.
   a   We can't pay until next month.
   b   We need more time to get used to our new office.
   c   We will send you the bill in a month's time.

2   Please find enclosed your statement for the month of March.
   a   We are sending details of all the transactions we made in March.
   b   We are informing you about what you owe us for March.
   c   We are sending the money we owe you for March.

3   The sum of £215.60 has been credited to your account.
   a   You will be expected to pay £215.60 from your account.
   b   We believe that you now have a total of £215.60 in your account.
   c   A payment of £215.60 has gone into your account.

4   I apologize for not clearing the balance earlier.
   a   Sorry I didn't pay you earlier.
   b   Sorry for not closing my account earlier.
   c   Sorry for the delay in replying to you.

5   Settlement of your February account is overdue.
   a   You paid us too much in February.
   b   We can't offer you a loan to pay your February account.
   c   You haven't paid us yet for February.

6   We ask you to bear with us.
   a   Please be patient.
   b   We need your custom.
   c   We would like you to pay us.

6.e   Make changes to the following letter so that it sounds more formal.

> Thanks for sending us £550 the other week, but don't
> forget you still owe us £2,000, which we want you to pay
> before the end of April. If you're having problems finding
> the money, why don't you give us a ring? We could
> arrange a different way for you to pay us.

6.f   Read the following letter requesting payment, and choose the best words from the options in brackets.

UK Cycles Ltd

Borough House
Borough Road
Cleveland TS1 3BA

Our Ref: HS 351

The Managing Director
Velo Sport AG
Karlstr. 45
O–5230 Sömerda

Account No. VS 301632

28 April 19 —

Dear Mr Janssen,

We wrote to you on 25 March concerning the above ¹(*account, bill*) for £2,700.00 which has now been outstanding ²(*for, since, about*) three months. When we agreed to offer you credit facilities we pointed out that it was essential to ³(*pay up, clear, handle*) accounts ⁴(*in, at, on*) the exact date, particularly as we generally do not ⁵(*allow, give, offer*) credit terms.

As you realize, delayed payments can create problems for us ⁶(*by, to, with*) our own suppliers, therefore we would appreciate it if you could either let us know why the ⁷(*account, credit, payment*) has not been cleared, or let us have a remittance ⁸(*within, for, during*) the next ten days.

We hope this receives your immediate attention.

Yours sincerely,

Helen Stuart

Helen Stuart (Mrs)
Accountant

6.g   Write a letter from Karl Janssen, Managing Director of Velo Sport, to Mrs Stuart.

- Thank her for her letters, and quote the dates.
- Explain that a fire at your Head Office has destroyed a lot of your computer data and has disrupted all correspondence with suppliers and customers. You need some time to get back to your normal routine.
- Request a further thirty days to settle.

6.h   Fill in the invoice with the information given below.

Ten Lotus pattern at £35 each, catalogue number L305; 20 Wedgwood at £43, catalogue number W218. Cost, Insurance, Freight is included in these prices. Less 15% trade discount.

GLASTON POTTERIES Ltd

Clayfield, Burnley BB10 1RQ
Tel: 0315 46125   Telex: 8801773   Fax: 0315 63182

INVOICE

No. 2087/85   Date: 9 May 19 —

To: J. F. Morreau
     1150 boulevard Calbert
     F–54015 Nancy Cedex

Your Order No. 3716

Quantity	Description	Cat. No.	£ each	£
_____	_____	_____	_____	____
_____	_____	_____	_____	____

		Total £	_____
		Less	_____ %

Payment due: _____
Signed: _J. Merton_ _____

6.i   Write a covering letter to accompany the above invoice. Inform Jean Morreau of the expected delivery date and remind him of the terms of the sale which are as follows:

Trade discount: 15%
Mode of payment: sight draft
Delivery period: 2 months

Complaints and adjustments

7

7.a Read this letter of complaint, and fill in the blanks with the correct verb taken from the list below.

have not arrived   found   was torn
have contacted   received   were damaged
have not had   showed
have informed   unpacked

C. R. Méndez S.A.
Avda. del Ejército 83   E–48015 Bilbao

The Sales Manager   15 October 19 —
Seymore Furniture Ltd.
Tib Street
Maidenhead
Berks. SL6 5DS

Dear Mr Harrison,

I am writing to complain about a shipment of tubular steel garden furniture we

(1)_____ yesterday against our invoice no. G 3190/1.

The crates (2)_____ on the outside, and looked as if they had been

roughly handled. When we (3)_____ them, we (4)_____ that

some of the chair legs were bent and rusty, and the fabric on the seating

(5)_____ , or (6)_____ signs of wear.

Two further crates from the consignment (7)_____ yet, so we

(8)_____ the opportunity of inspecting them. I (9)_____ the

shipping company that we cannot accept this consignment from you, and they

(10)_____ your insurers.

As we will be unable to retail this consignment in our stores, we are returning
the shipment to you carriage forward, and we shall expect a full refund.

Yours sincerely,

C. A. Méndez

C. R. Méndez
Managing Director

7.b Read the following extracts from letters of complaint. Write out the verbs in either the simple past, (e.g. *he worked*) or the present perfect, (e.g. *he has worked*).

1 Last year we (not/have) _____ any serious complaints from our

   clients, but this year we (already/received) _____ over twenty.

2 This is not the first time that we (have) _____ problems with the

   shipping company. Three months ago they (lose) _____ a

   consignment completely and they still (not/find) _____ out what
   happened to it.

3 I (look) _____ into the problem, and it appears that the catalogue

   (be) _____ out of date.

4 I (receive) _____ a consignment of furniture from you last week

   which we (order) _____ on May 12.

5 The error (be) _____ due to a fault in the computer system which

   we now (put) _____ right.

6 Our engineers (recently/find) _____ a fault with the batch of

   hard disk drives that we (manufacture) _____ in June and July
   last year.

7 I am writing to apologize for the defective items you (receive) _____

   last month, and to inform you that we (credit) _____ the sum of
   £342.67 to your account.

8 Our accounts department (inform) _____ me that we

   (not/yet/receive) _____ payment for the items we

   (send) _____

9 We (not have) _____ any business from Winford & Co.

   since we (make) _____ an error with an invoice.

10 We (lose) _____ a number of orders since we (start)

   _____ having problems with the switchboard.

7.c   Which words in each pair, if any, are not spelled correctly?

1 a faithfully
   b faithfuly

2 a address
   b adress

3 a bussiness
   b business

4 a clerk
   b clark

5 a check
   b cheque

6 a catalog
   b catalogue

7.d   Compare the two lists of expressions commonly used in complaints. Match the informal phrases in the first list with their formal equivalents in the second.

1   it's not our fault
2   you should make it right
3   we want our money back
4   you have to pay when the goods are returned to you
5   we will sue you
6   you made a mistake
7   we won't buy anything from you again
8   the goods are rubbish
9   we're complaining about
10 why don't you pay attention?

a   we are sending the consignment to you carriage forward
b   we are not responsible for the error
c   we would like to complain about . . . .
d   we will have to take legal action
e   you seem to have made an error
f   the products are not satisfactory
g   we will not re-order
h   you have not followed our instructions
i   please correct the error
j   we would like a refund

7.e   Read 7.a again and write a reply from Mr Harrison to Mr Méndez.

■ Thank him for his letter, and apologize for the damage.
■ Explain that the goods were not old stock, but the damage appears to have happened while the goods were being transported. Assure him that you will deal with the transport company.
■ Say that you will accept the goods carriage forward, and that you will send the refund by banker's draft as soon as you receive them.
■ Close the letter in an appropriate manner.

7.f   Complete each unfinished sentence, so that it means the same as the one before it.

Example
We had a lot of problems. Nevertheless we solved them.
Although we had a lot of problems, we solved them.

1   If we had known they were going out of business, we would not have given them credit.

Had we _____

2   We wrote to you on 5 January. Our letter complained about poor workmanship.

In our letter _____(one sentence)

3   You have made an error on your September statement.

An error _____

4   'Please contact our accounts department,' the secretary said.

The secretary told me _____

5   We want the consignment returned, before we give you a refund.

Could _____

6   We will deal with the problem as soon as we have the details.

The problem _____

7   The credit is too large for us to allow.

The credit is so _____

8   They offered to exchange the goods and give us a discount.

Not only _____

9   Fill out the details on the credit application form and return it to us.

After you _____

7.g Use the *a*, or *the*, or leave the spaces blank in this letter of complaint.

ISTITUTO DI MEDICINA
Viale Bracci
I–61001 Siena

15 June 19 —

The Sales Manager
Nihon Instruments
12–18 Wakakusa-cho
Hagashi-Osaka-Shi
Osaka-fu
Japan

Dear Mr Toda,

AWB 4156/82

We are writing to point out that (1)_____ above delivery, which
arrived yesterday, was (2)_____ week late. This is (3)_____
second time we have had to write to you on this subject, and we
cannot allow (4)_____ situation to continue. We have already
explained that it is essential for (5)_____ medical equipment to
arrive on (6)_____ due date as (7)_____ late delivery could
create (8)_____ very serious problem.

Unless we have (9)_____ absolute assurance that you can
guarantee (10)_____ promptness of all future deliveries, we will
have to look for another supplier. We will want your confirmation
before we place our next order.

Yours sincerely,

Carlo Lotti
Carlo Lotti
Head of Administration

7.h Write the letter from Mr Hirio Toda, the Sales Manager of the above company, to Mr
Lotti, politely explaining that the orders were sent to your factory address, not your
administrative address, as above, and explain what that means in terms of delay.
However, sympathize with Mr Lotti and suggest a solution to the problem.

Credit

8

8.a Read this letter requesting credit, and fill in the blanks with the correct verb taken from the list below.

place	began	may be approached	have been cleared
have been trading	has passed	would be settled	had been established

---

D. L. Cromer Ltd
Central Trading Estate
Staines
Middlesex TW19 4UP

The Sales Manager   12 May 19 —
Antonio Medina S.L.
C/Sagasta 1156
Barcelona 08317

Dear Mr Medina,

We (1)_____ with you for the past year and during that time our accounts (2)_____ by letter of credit. However, when we (3)_____ our association with you, you mentioned that once a business relationship (4)_____, our accounts (5)_____ by 60–day bill of exchange, documents against acceptance. We feel that sufficient time (6)_____ to allow this arrangement to be effected.

Please let us know before we (7)_____ our next order, if these new payment terms are acceptable.

I enclose details of two referees, who (8)_____ should you require trade references, and look forward to hearing from you.

Yours sincerely,

David Arnold

David Arnold
Accountant

Encs.

8.b Complete each unfinished sentence, using the passive voice, so that it means the same as the one before it.

Example
We have settled our accounts up to now by letter of credit.
Our accounts *have been settled up to now by letter of credit*.

1 A supplier only grants credit facilities if a customer can satisfy a number of requirements.

Credit facilities _____

_____

2 We would like to confirm that you will make settlement against monthly statements.

We would like to confirm that settlement _____

_____

3 We cannot offer open account terms, as we price our products very competitively.

We cannot offer open account terms, as our _____

_____

4 We will include the enclosed invoice on your next statement.

The enclosed _____

5 Our bank has advised us that they have credited the proceeds of our letter of credit to your account.

Our bank has advised us that the proceeds _____

_____

6 We have had to remind this firm several times to settle their accounts.

This firm _____

7 Would you please tell us if anyone has ever taken court action against this firm?

Would you please tell us if court _____

8 We have now completed our investigation into Falcon Retailers.

Our _____

9 LDM Ltd brought an action against the firm in 1979.

An _____

10 Could you tell us whether we can rely on them to settle their accounts promptly?

Could you tell us whether they _____

8.c In the following sentences, the word in italics is not very appropriate for formal correspondence. Choose a more suitable alternative from the list.

inform   overdue   request   promptly   sufficient
elapsed   confidential   acceptable   competitive   settle

1 Thank you for forwarding the documents so *quickly*.
2 We feel that *enough* time has *passed* for you to *pay*.
3 I am writing to *ask for* open account facilities.
4 We remind you that this information is highly *secret*.
5 Your quarterly settlement is three weeks *late*.
6 We are pleased to tell you that the credit facilities you asked for are *fine*.
7 Our prices are very *low*.

8.d Complete the following request for a reference with the correct prepositions.

Antonio Medina S.L.
C/Sagasta 1156   Barcelona 08317

The Credit Controller   18 May 19 —
British Suppliers PLC
Hoxteth House
Wrights Way
Glasgow G12 8QQ

Dear Mr MacFee,

We are writing (1)_____ you (2)_____
the recommendation (3)_____ Mr David Arnold,
the accountant (4)_____ D.L. Cromer Ltd.
(5)_____ Staines, Middlesex. He advised us to
contact you as a referee, concerning credit facilities,
which his company has asked us (6)_____.

Could you confirm that the company settles
(7)_____ due dates, and is sound enough to meet
credits of (8)_____ to £5,000 in transactions.

We would be grateful (9)_____ a reply
(10)_____ your earliest possible convenience.

Yours sincerely,

P. Gómez

P. Gómez (Mrs)
Sales Manageress

8.e   Use the words below to complete this letter from a referee.

information	credit-worthiness	statements
customer	confidence	limit
balances	due	

British Suppliers PLC

Hoxteth House, Wrights Way
Glasgow G12 8QQ

The Sales Manager   27 May 19 —
Antonio Media S.L.
C/Sagasta 1156
Barcelona 08317

Dear Mrs Gómez,

I refer to your letter of May 18 concerning the
(1)_____ of D. L. Cromer Ltd.

The company has been a (2)_____ of
ours for a number of years, and although their credit
(3)_____ has not reached the level you
mentioned, we have found that they always cleared
their (4)_____ on the
(5)_____ dates, settling them on
quarterly (6)_____ .

We trust you will treat this (7)_____ in
the strictest (8)_____ .

Yours sincerely,

G. MacFee

G. MacFee
Credit Controller

8.f   Write the letter from Patricia Gómez to Mr Arnold, informing him that the references are favourable and offering him the credit facilities he requested.

Banking

9

9.a Read the sentences below. Then find the verb from the list which best fits each situation.

explain   promise   apologize   thank
admit   refuse   suggest   advise

Example
I am grateful to you for sending the shipping documents so promptly. _____thank_____

1 Why don't you think it over for a few days and then get back to me?

   _____

2 I'm afraid we cannot extend your overdraft. _____

3 I think you should consider our terms before making a decision.

   _____

4 I'll definitely let you have the details tomorrow. _____

5 It appears that we made a mistake on your October statement. _____

6 You understand that the bank will want about 120% in securities to cover this credit.

   _____

7 We are very sorry for the delay in replying to your request. _____

9.b Change the sentences from Exercise 9.a into reported speech, using the appropriate verb. Add other words as necessary, in order to make complete sentences.

Example
I am grateful to you for sending the shipping documents so promptly.
She thanked (me) for sending the shipping documents promptly.

9.c The following is a covering letter from a bank, informing a company that a letter of credit has been opened for them. Choose the correct expressions from the list below to fill in the gaps.

inform   charges   documents   draw
acting   valid   settle   opened

Banque de Lyon
500 boulevard Jobert   69000 Lyon

The Accountant   8 July 19 —
Guy Lussac
80 rue Gaspart–André
69003 Lyon (Rhône)

Dear Sir

L/C No. 340895/AGL

We are (1)_____ on behalf of the Eastland Bank, London,
and would like to (2)_____ you that the above
documentary credit for 45,000 FF has been (3)_____ in
your favour by your customers Mercury Data Ltd. The credit is
(4)_____ until 12 August and all bank (5)_____
have been paid.

Please bring the following (6)_____ to the above address:

    Air Waybill

    Invoice for full value of the sale c.i.f. London

    Insurance Certificate

    Certificate of Origin

Would you also (7)_____ a sight draft for the full amount
of the invoice on us so that we can (8)_____ this account.
Thank you in advance.

Yours faithfully

Paul Diderot

Paul Diderot
Documentary Credits Manager

9.d   Rewrite the following sentences so that they sound more polite.

Example
We want a loan.
Can you offer us a loan?

1   Repay the credit within the next ten days.

2   Send us an application form.

3   How much is the interest?

4   We want a six-month credit.

5   When do we repay the loan?

6   We don't want an account with this bank any more.

9.e   Use the correct form of the word in brackets.

Example
Lack of capital will _____ the project. (danger)
Lack of capital will endanger the project.

1   The exporter opens a letter of credit by _____ an application form.   (complete)

2   The cheque should be made _____ to International Crafts Ltd.   (pay)

3   The shipping documents include bill of lading _____ and invoice.   (insure)

4   I am pleased to inform you that your _____ has now been extended to £4,000.   (overdraw)

5   I am writing to acknowledge _____ of your letter, dated 5 April.   (receive)

6   You will receive _____ of the agreement from our bank.   (confirm)

7   With _____ to our telephone conversation yesterday, I am writing to confirm our agreement.   (refer)

8 Loans can be extended only by _____ with the branch manager. (arrange)

9 Your _____ should appear twice on the document. (sign)

10 We need a loan to secure the _____ of our company. (expand)

9.f Read the following dialogue between a bank manager, John Steele, and a customer, Richard Grey.

Manager Good afternoon, Mr Grey. Now, how can I help you?

Customer Well, I know my company's been going through a bad time recently, but I would like to expand the fleet by buying another two lorries. I wonder if you could extend my loan to cover the investment?

Manager I'm afraid we can't extend your existing loan, but we may be able to offer a bridging loan. How much would you need?

Customer Probably around £30,000 to buy two second-hand vehicles. I'm sure that the revenue from the extra lorries would allow me to repay you within a year.

Manager What can you offer as security for the loan?

Customer Just the lorries themselves.

Manager Well, unfortunately, I am not in a position to make an independent decision – I shall have to consult with our directors first – but I promise I will speak to them this week, and let you know as soon as possible.

Customer Thank you very much.

Now, as Mr Steele, relate the above conversation in a memo to the directors. Try to use some of the reporting verbs from Exercises 9.a and 9.b where appropriate, but ensure that you only report the details which would be of interest to the directors. Start as follows:

I had a meeting with a customer, Richard Grey, on the 17 September . . .

9.g Owing to an economic recession, you have doubts about Mr Grey's proposal. Also your directors now insist that all loans should be covered by negotiable securities, such as shares or bonds. Write a letter to Mr Grey, explaining that credit has been refused, but advise him that there are other sources he could try, e.g. finance houses. Nevertheless, warn him that their interest rates could be rather higher than the bank's.

Your address: The Counties Bank, 60 City Road, Salford M5 4WT.

Customer's address: Richard Grey, Grey Transport Ltd., 350 Dock Street, Salford M6 3WT.

Agents and agencies

10

10.a Read the two passages spoken by Susan Payne and her new secretary. Fill in the spaces with the correct form of *make* or *do*.

I don't know what we can (1) _____ about this new secretary. She can't (2) _____ even the simplest things right. Last week, she (3) _____ an appointment for me to see one of our most important agents when I was on holiday, and she (4) _____ the most terrible typing errors too – she sent a buyer an invoice for £200 instead of £20,000, which I fortunately saw just in time, and I (5) _____ her (6) _____ it again. But I can't see how we can (7) _____ business and (8) _____ a profit if we have people like that working for us.

I had a really terrible day at the office. I managed to (9) _____ quite a lot of work in the morning, and I (10) _____ my new boss endless cups of coffee, and I (11) _____ all the filing. But she didn't seem to be at all happy. After lunch I (12) _____ a few more letters, and I was a bit tired, so I (13) _____ a few small mistakes. She was absolutely furious and (14) _____ such a fuss! I told her I was (15) _____ my best and that seemed to (16) _____ her even more angry. I think she ought to learn to (17) _____ her own typing.

10.b Complete the boxes with the missing word from the sentences below to find the 'key' word down.

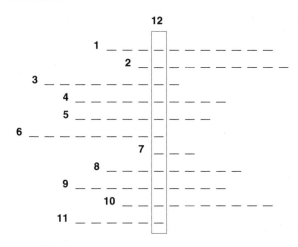

ACROSS

1   A _____ is someone who buys and sells shares for a client on the Stock Exchange.

2   _____ houses receive goods from abroad and often make all the import arrangements before selling the goods on to a client.

3   A _____ _____ only sells products from his principal and does not sell competing products. (2 words: 4,5)

4   An agent who sells products on a _____ basis makes a certain amount of money for each item sold.

5   A _____ is someone who supplies products to an agent.

6   In non-recourse _____ , a firm buys up outstanding invoices and claims the debts.

7   Commission may be worked out on c.i.f. invoice values, or _____ invoice values.

8   The _____ markets are where items like coffee, cocoa, and rubber are traded on behalf of clients.

9   Agents who take the risk of being liable for customers' debts may receive a _____ _____ commission. (2 words: 3,7)

10 An agent who sells products on his _____ _____ can set his own prices and profit margins. (2 words: 3,7)

11 A prospective agent may need to be convinced that there is a _____ for the principal's products.

12 'Key' word (DOWN): the basis on which an agent sells your products but does not own them himself, and makes a profit from commission only.

10.c Using a word from column **A** and a word from column **B**, complete each sentence with a phrasal verb which means the same as the word or phrase in brackets.

The first one has been done as an example.

A	B
take	in
take	out
do	down
fill	on
back	over
turn	up
work	without
make	off
make	out
cut	up

1 Find out what the real sales figures for last year were. You can't

just _____ them _____ ! (invent)

2 Please _____ the cheque _____ to the M&G Pensions and Annuity Company. (write down the name of the payee)

3 We can't afford to employ temporary staff for two days; you will just have

to _____ _____ a secretary until Monday. (manage without)

4 The small company, which had suffered from bad management, was _____

_____ by a larger one, and all the directors were fired. (gained control of)

5 We offer all our agents extensive advice, and _____ them _____ with a full range of financial services. (support)

6 We must _____ _____ their offer to act as agents for us, because they have not been in business long enough. (refuse)

7 The company was expanding, so they decided to _____ _____ a hundred new workers. (employ)

8 It's going to take a few days to _____ _____ all the details of the contract. (calculate)

9 Please _____ _____ the enclosed application form and return it to us. (complete)

10 We were talking on the phone and we were suddenly _____ _____, so I'll have to ring him back. (disconnected)

10.d   Read the following letter, offering an agency, and choose the best words from the
options in brackets.

Grazioli S.p.A.
Via Gradenigo 134
50133 Firenze

Grassmann AG
Lindenweg 18
D–1000 Berlin 12

23 October 19 —

Dear Mr Grassmann,

You were recommended to us by the German Chamber of Commerce,
who [1](*said, told, spoke*) you might be interested in representing an Italian
glass manufacturing company in your country.

We have a number of agencies in other European countries who receive
products on [2](*commission, consignment, approval*), then sell them on a six
per cent commission on ex-works prices. These are [3](*single, unique, sole*)
agencies which means that only we supply them, and they represent only
us in this line.

Generally, their customers [4](*settle, agree, deal*) all accounts with us, then
we supply them direct on invoices received from the agent.

In most cases we offer a [5](*test, proof, trial*) agency for one year, and if
the results are good, we [6](*export, entend, expand*) the agency on a
further two-year contract. We would [7](*offer, suggest, invite*) you support
through advertising, brochures, and leaflets in German, the [8](*cost, value,
worth*) of this being shared between us.

Our market [9](*researchers, reporters, informers*) tell us there is an
increasing demand for our line of products in your country, so it will not
be difficult to sell our wares.

If you would be interested in an agency of this type, we can send you a
standard agreement, giving you more details of our terms. Meanwhile, we
are enclosing our [10](*actual, present, current*) catalogue.

Yours sincerely,

P. Grazioli

P. Grazioli
Chairman

Encl.

10.e Choose the phrase or sentence from the options which would be most appropriate when replying to the letter in 10.d.

1 a Thanks very much for your letter the other day . . .
  b I was delighted when I received your recent communication . . .
  c Thank you for your letter of 23 October . . .

2 a We would be interested in representing you, but not on a sole agency basis, as this would restrict our sales.
  b No way could we go ahead on a sole agency basis, as we've got to sell a lot.
  c Were it not for the sole agency basis, your proposal might have been received more favourably.

3 a We want a cut of 10 per cent and three quarters of the ads paid by you.
  b A 10 per cent commission on ex-works prices and 75 per cent support in advertising are the basis on which an agreement might be negotiated.
  c Our usual terms are a 10 per cent commission on ex-works prices and 75 per cent of the advertising costs.

4 a Everyone in the German market knows us.
  b We are held in high regard in, and have extensive knowledge of, the German market.
  c We have extensive connections in the German market.

5 a We were overwhelmed by the superlative quality of the products in your catalogue.
  b The products in your catalogue look really good.
  c We were impressed by the high quality of your products.

6 a If you are able to revise your terms, we would be interested in seeing a draft contract.
  b Subject to a satisfactory revision of terms, a draft contract would be worthy of consideration.
  c If you can have a look at your terms again, pop a contract in the post and we'll have a look at it.

10.f Read the letter opposite from a company asking to act as a buying agency. Choose the correct words from the list below.

offer	commission	principals	rates	documentation	freight
del credere	recommendation	terms	factory	manufacturers	brochure

10.g Write a reply to Mr Kobelt from Cristina Neves. In your letter include the following information:

- Thank Mr Kobelt for his letter.
- Say that you are interested in his proposals because there is an increasing demand for precision tools in Portugal; suggest that you could accept either 3 per cent commission on c.i.f. values, or the 2.5 per cent del credere commission.
- You would like to know if they can act as clearing and forwarding agents, offering a door-to-door facility.
- Check that they will send references from other companies they act for.
- Suggest that, if this is possible, one of the directors could meet them to discuss a contract.
- Close the letter as appropriate.

The Kobelt Agency
Brauneggerstr. 618
D–4400 Münster

The Buying Manager
Portuguese Industrial Importers
Rua dos Santos, 179
1200 Lisboa
Portugal

24 June 19 —

Dear Mrs Neves,

We are writing to you on the (1)_____ of the Portuguese Chamber of
Commerce who informed us that you were looking for a buying agent for
precision tools in this country.

We have been in this trade for over twenty years and have close contacts with
the major (2)_____ both here and overseas.

If we may, we would like to give you a brief outline of the (3)_____ we
work on. Generally, we place orders for our (4)_____ with our suppliers,
and our customers settle direct with the manufacturer. In addition we arrange all
costs, insurance and (5)_____ facilities for the client handling consignments
from the (6)_____ to the port/airport of the importer's country.

As we have dealt with these agencies for a number of years, we can offer you
their most competitive (7)_____ for shipment. In addition we would take
care of all (8)_____ , including customs formalities.

As a rule we operate on a 4.5 per cent (9)_____ on c.i.f. values, but if
credit is involved, we could offer (10)_____ services for an additional
2.5 per cent commission, pending the usual inquiries.

If you are interested in this (11)_____ we can assure you of first class,
efficient service. Meanwhile, do not hesitate to contact us for any more
information. Please find enclosed our (12)_____ giving you full details of
our company.

We look forward to hearing from you in due course.

Yours sincerely,

M. Kobelt

M. Kobelt
Managing Director

Enc.

Transport

11

11.a Complete the sentences with one of the following words or phrases: *if, unless, when, in case*.

1 Our suppliers have told us that the goods were in perfect condition

_____ they left the factory.

2 The ferry takes three hours to cross the Channel _____ the weather is very bad, in which case it takes longer.

3 It is important to be adequately insured _____ a consignment is damaged in transit.

4 The banks will not accept non-negotiable waybills as evidence of shipment

_____ they are instructed to do so.

5 The SS Africa sailed from Tilbury on June 26, and we will let you know

_____ it arrives in Nigeria.

6 _____ you want to reserve a container on the SS Orient, please complete the enclosed forms and return them to us by March 15.

7 The SS Sheraton will be available for charter _____ she returns from Australia at the end of the month.

11.b Complete each unfinished sentence in this exercise so that it means the same as the one before it.

Example
The weather was bad, so the ship was delayed.
If *the weather hadn't been bad, the ship wouldn't have been delayed*.

1 The firm did not receive any compensation because the goods weren't insured.

If the goods _____

2 The shipment arrived late because the dockers went on strike.

If the dockers _____

3 The company did not send the shipment by rail, so the goods arrived late.

The goods wouldn't _____

4 The goods were not perishable, so they were sent by rail.

If the goods _____

5 The consignor did not receive any compensation because the carriers were not negligent.

The consignor would _____

6 These problems arose because we did not use our normal forwarding agents.

If we _____

7 The records and tapes were damaged because they had not been packed properly.

If the records _____

11.c Make words from the jumbled letters and match them with the definitions in the sentences below.

a RNTOANCEI EVESSSL   h ALTCIB GENACHXE
b RTYDI   i CNEEEGNGLI
c ILBI FO GANDIL   j NRALECIG GATEN
d AWBYILL   k CATSRE
e EIFHRGT ONCTACU   l AERFGIL
f GNISCOEEN   m PLIHBREASE ODOGS
g KCOD PIRTECE   n IFCTERECITA FO IIGNOR

1 Someone who ensures that goods are cleared through customs. (2 words)
2 Items like fruit, butter, and meat that can go bad during transit. (2 words)
3 What a bill of lading may be marked if goods are damaged. (1 word)
4 The equivalent of a consignment note for air transport. (1 word)
5 Carelessness. (1 word)
6 The person who receives goods being transported. (1 word)
7 What is written on a consignment that can be broken easily. (1 word)
8 Ships on which goods are kept in huge steel boxes. (2 words)
9 A shipping document giving ownership to the person named on it. (3 words)
10 An invoice sent by a shipping company stating their charges. (2 words)
11 Wooden boxes in which items may be packed. (1 word)
12 The organization through which ships can be chartered. (2 words)
13 A document stating what is in a consignment and where it is from. (3 words)
14 A document stating that goods are stored and awaiting shipment. (2 words)

11.d Complete this letter enquiring about a forwarding agent's charges with the correct prepositions.

Note: forwarding agents will collect a consignment and make all the arrangements for shipment to the customer, including documentation if necessary.

Möbelhaus AG

Reichenbergerstrasse 401   Berlin 61

Dietmann Spedition GmbH
Kanalstrasse 190
Berlin 31

10 November 19 —

Dear Mr Dietmann,

You were recommended (1)_____ us (2)_____ Gebrauchte Stilmobel, our associates, (3)_____ whom you have operated as forwarding agents.

We are looking (4)_____ a reliable company to handle our deliveries (5)_____ Europe, taking care (6)_____ documentation and making sure (7)_____ a safe delivery, as many (8)_____ our products become worthless if damaged.

Enclosed you will find a list representing a consignment we wish to send (9)_____ Lausanne (10)_____ Switzerland. We would like it to be delivered there (11)_____ road (12)_____ a door-to-door basis. Could you let us have your quotation, and if it is competitive, we can assure you (13)_____ further business (14)_____ the future.

Yours sincerely,

R. Behrendt

R. Behrendt
Transport Supervisor

Encl.

Here is the reply from the forwarding agents to Möbelhaus AG. Put the words and phrases from the letter in the correct order, and add punctuation where necessary.

Example
Thank you / of 15 May / yesterday / which we received / for your letter
Thank you for your letter of 15 May, which we received yesterday.

Dietmann Spedition GmbH
Kanalstrasse 190   Berlin 31

The Transport Supervisor   12 November 19 —
Möbelhaus AG
Reichenbergerstrasse 401
Berlin 61

Dear Mr Behrendt,

Thank you / of 10 November / in which you asked about changes / for your letter / in Europe / of your goods / for the transportation

_____

_____

all transport, customs, and documentation charges / We are enclosing / for shipments / our tariff list / which includes

_____

_____

safe transport / for manufacturers / as we have a lot of experience in handling products / We can certainly promise

_____

_____

you / we will be pleased to help / any further enquiries / If you have

_____

please return / Meanwhile / the enclosed 'Freight Forwarding Instructions Form' / should you decide / for your consignment / to use Dietmann Spedition / to Switzerland

_____

_____

Yours sincerely,

J. Dietmann
J. Dietmann

Enc.

11.f Write a fax based on the following information.

Sender Mr J. Merton, Glaston Potteries, Clayfield, Burnley BB10 1RQ.

Date 13 June 19—

Receiver National Containers Limited, 318 Leadenhall St., London EC1 1DR

You have a number of European deliveries over the next few months which you want National Containers to handle. Consignments consist of fragile crockery. Average crate measures 187 × 172 × 165 cm. Approx 35 kg. each. You want door-to-door delivery. Ask for quotation and schedules. You also want immediate information concerning documentation.

11.g Now read the faxed answer to your fax, from Glaston Potteries. Choose the best word from the words in brackets.

FAX: 071 625 1397   DATE: 14 June 19 —   TIME: 16.21

National Containers Limited
318 LEADENHALL STREET   LONDON EC1 1DR

To: Fax 0315 63182   **Date:** 14 June 19 —
Glaston Potteries Ltd
Clayfield
Burnley BB10 1RQ

Dear Mr Merton,

In reply to your fax of the [1](*before, over, above*) date, we are sending you details of our shipping [2](*timetables, schedules, programs*) and freight rates, so they should [3](*arrive, reach, deliver*) you by tomorrow.

With regard to the [4](*certification, documentation, paper*) you asked for, we [5](*suggest, advise, warn*) you use our Combined Transport Bill as the goods will then be covered by road, Ro-Ro ferry, and road again. We are also sending [6](*down, on, up*) our Export Cargo Packing Instructions which should be [7](*brought, handed, put*) to our driver when he calls. Consignment will be delivered to our [8](*post, camp, depot*) for consolidation, and you will be [9](*charged, accounted, paid*) at the very competitive groupage rates.

We will take the usual [10](*duties, responsibilities, care*) for handling cargo, but suggest you take all risk insurance cover on a door-to-door [11](*term, basis, ground*).

Please let us know [12](*as, if, when*) there are any other details you require.

Yours sincerely,

Brian Close

Brian Close
Freight Manager

Insurance

12

12.a   Put the following verbs into the infinitive form, (e.g. *to do*) or the gerund, (e.g. *doing*).

1   The headmaster suggested (get) _____ Personal Accident Insurance for

the students who were planning (go) _____ on a school skiing holiday.

2   It's well worth (get) _____ comprehensively insured so that you don't risk

(lose) _____ a great deal of money.

3   The company were not able (afford) _____ the high premiums, so they

decided (ask) _____ another company for a quote.

4   Our insurers seemed (want) _____ (avoid) _____ (pay)

_____ the claim until the last possible moment.

5   The insurance company offered (pay) _____ £6300 of the claim for the

damage caused by the fire and advised the company (have) _____ the
building rewired.

6   Westway Insurance refused (meet) _____ the claim for the damage

caused by the burst pipe, and said the claimant had failed (read) _____ the
policy properly.

7   We would like (arrange) _____ an all risk open cover policy for our

chinaware shipments which we intend (export) _____ over the next three
months.

8   I enclose the claim which you asked us (send) _____, and I look forward to

(hear) _____ from you.

12.b   Match the sentences in section **A** with the meanings in section **B**.

A

1   I regret to say that you did not renew the policy in time.
2   I regret saying that you did not renew the policy in time.
3   The underwriters remembered paying Mr Goodman for the damaged consignments.
4   The underwriters remembered to pay Mr Goodman for the damaged consignments.
5   The vessel stopped unloading the containers after the accident.
6   The vessel stopped to unload the containers after the accident.

B

a   The underwriters knew that they had paid Mr Goodman.
b   There was an accident, so they decided to unload the containers.
c   I'm sorry I accused you of forgetting to renew the policy.
d   There was an accident, so they didn't unload any more containers.
e   I'm afraid to say that you were responsible for forgetting to renew the policy.
f   Mr Goodman did not have to remind the underwriters to pay.

12.c   Complete the following sentences with the missing words.

1   An i_____ company indemnifies clients against loss. (9)

2   Underwriters at Lloyds work in groups called s_____ . (10)

3   An insurance p_____ is a contract taken out to protect someone against risks. (6)

4   A client is i_____ against loss of damage when he has an insurance policy. (7)

5   A p_____ is the amount of money paid to an insurance company for cover. (7)

6   L_____ list is a daily newspaper about shipping movements and cargo markets. (6)

7   A p_____ form is completed by a firm or person who wants cover. (8)

8   A c_____ form is sent to an insurance company after a client has suffered a loss. (6)

9   Under f_____ bonds, companies can insure themselves against dishonest employees. (8)

12.d Read the following letter and choose the best words from the options in brackets.

HUMBOLT EXPORTERS LTD

Exode House · 115 Tremona Road · Southampton SO9 4XY

International Insurance PLC   15 February 19 —
153 Western Road
Brighton
Sussex

Dear Sir,

We are a [1](*grand, large, wide*) export company [2](*dealing, coping, managing*) with merchandise [3](*who, which, what*) we ship [4](*in, to, towards*) Europe and North America. We [5](*want, would like, request*) to know if you can [6](*suggest, supply, give*) us with a quotation for a comprehensive policy, [7](*assuring, protecting, covering*) our warehouse at Dock Road, Southampton.

The policy would [8](*consist, contain, include*) fire, flood, theft, burglary, and the usual contingencies affecting this [9](*form, kind, variety*) of enterprise. At any one time, there may be about £250,000 in stock on the [10](*premises, grounds, floors*).

If you can offer us [11](*competing, competition, competitive*) rates, we will [12](*think, imagine, consider*) further policies with you on our other interests.

We look forward to hearing from you [13](*soon, presently, immediately*).

Yours faithfully,

Peter Hind

Peter Hind
Company Secretary

12.e Due to a malfunctioning word processor, the following two letters have been mixed up. One is from an engineering company enquiring about a staff pension scheme. The other is the reply from the insurance company. Re-arrange the paragraphs and phrases to form the two letters. Write a, b, c, etc. in the boxes opposite, showing where each part of both letters should be.

a Yours faithfully,
J Steward
Company Secretary

b Please contact me, in the meantime, if you have anything else you would like to discuss.

c The enclosed booklet, PS 134, will give you details of the type of policy I think would suit you. The minimum age for joining would be 18, with a retirement plan at 55 for women and 60 for men.

d UK Engineeering PLC
Brunel House
Brunel Street
Liverpool L2 2ER

e Finally, as well as choosing a retirement pension, we would also like a policy which would include life insurance, so that in the event of an early death, the insured's dependants would get a lump sum in benefit payment.

f Thank you for writing to us.

g On this basis, we would estimate those eligible at the present time to number about 300 or so, with ages ranging from apprentices of 16 to skilled operatives and administrators in their early 50s.

h I am replying to your letter of 15 September concerning a contributory staff pension scheme for your employees.

i The Company Secretary
UK Engineering PLC
Brunel House
Brunel Street
Liverpool L2 2ER

j I can arrange for an agent to call on you at any time, and will contact you in a few days after you have had time to consider this proposal.

k We are a large engineering company with a staff of 400 including administrative and shop-floor staff. We are contacting a number of insurance companies to enquire about a contributory staff pension scheme to cover people who have been with us for over a year.

l If you have such a scheme, please let us have details, and we could possibly arrange a meeting with one of your agents.

m Dear Sir/Madam,

n Policies Manager
Associated Insurance PLC
153/8 Cressy Street
Liverpool L2 3EB

o Employee contributions could be arranged at 7 per cent, and the policy incorporates life insurance and benefit payment in the event of death.

p Dear Mr Steward,

q Yours sincerely,
Ralph Meeker
Policies Manager
Encl

r 19 September 19—

s 15 September 19—

t Associated Insurance
153/8 Cressy Street
Liverpool L2 3EB

12.f Read the following letter to an insurance broker enquiring about marine insurance policies, and fill in the blanks with the correct prepositions.

UK Engineering PLC
Brunel House
Brunel Street
Liverpool L2 2ER

Sugden and Able
Insurance Brokers
63 Grover Street
Manchester M5 6LD

1 May 19 —

Dear Sir/Madam,

We are a large engineering company exporting machine parts worldwide, and we have set up contracts (1)_____ Middle Eastern customers (2)_____ the next two years.

As these parts are similar (3)_____ nature and are going (4)_____ the same destination over this period, we thought it might be less expensive if we insured them, (5)_____ an all risk basis, (6)_____ a time policy.

We would appreciate it if you could give us any information (7)_____ this type (8)_____ cover and how it operates.

Yours faithfully,

Jack Turner

Jack Turner
Shipping Manager

12.g Mr A. Able, the Director of Sugden and Able, has left the following message for his secretary. Read what he says and write out the letter for Mr Able to sign.

> Tell him that underwriters offer 2 types of insurance for his requirements:
>
> 1 Floating policy – will cover all shipments with a maximum amount, and can be renewed when necessary.
>
> 2 Open cover – the shipper informs the underwriter when the shipment is made and renews the policy after shipment.

12.h Read the following notes about a warehouse fire. Write a letter from Mr Peter Hind of Humbolt Exporters to International Insurance PLC (see 12.d) telling them about the fire, and asking them to send a claims form.

Inform insurers of fire.

Warehouse fire: 8 July 19 —

Cause: electrical fault

Damage to textiles stored for shipment

Approximate amount of damage: £7,000

Insurance policy number: 439178/D

Electronic correspondence 13

13.a Read the following passage about telex, fax, and email.

The telex looks much like a typewriter, it acts as a printed phone message, sending messages directly over phone lines. Once the sender receives a code showing that a connection has been made, he/she can then type a message and receive an immediate reply. Although messages can be sent in normal English, there are a number of abbreviations that are commonly used. If a mistake is made, five Xs are used to show a correction, (e.g. WE AHVEXXXXX HAVE SENT YOUR ORDER). At the end of a message, a + sign is normally used, and a + ? sign means that the sender wants a reply, or confirmation, or will send a further message.

The fax system, like the telex, uses phone lines, and the numbers are similar to telephone numbers, with country codes, area codes, and the subscriber's number. The fax is one of the fastest growing areas of the electronics market, and numerous models are available. Some of these are faster than others, and some can reproduce photographs more accurately than others. Almost any kind of typed or written document can be transmitted by fax, whether it is an estimate, a design, or a photograph. Charges are measured in telephone units.

Electronic mail requires a computer and a modem which can convert typed messages and send them over the phone line. Subscribers can have a mailbox, which can receive and pass on messages from all over the world. Apart from being fast, reliable and accessible, one sender can reach hundreds of receivers at one time, on a VDU (visual display unit), with the screen showing the message.

13.b Find a word or phrase in the above text that means:

1 shortened forms of words
2 additional
3 nearly the same as
4 a person who regularly
   pays for a service
5 a large number of
6 precisely
7 sent
8 needs
9 change
10 a secret code word

13.c Complete the sentences below, by putting the adjective in brackets into the comparative or superlative forms, where necessary. In some cases, you will need to change the adjective into an adverb first.

Example
I think this must be (incomprehensible) telex I've ever seen.
I think this must be the most incomprehensible telex I've ever seen.

Photographs and diagrams can be transmitted very (accurate) by fax.
Photographs and diagrams can be transmitted very accurately by fax.

1 I've just received (long) fax I've ever had in my life.
2 In certain developing countries, telexes are (reliable) than faxes.
3 She couldn't read the fax very (good) so she asked them to send another copy (immediate), and the second one was much (good).
4 Our latest telex machine is one of (efficient) available, and it is also (cheap) than our competitors'.
5 Although some messages can be sent (efficient) by electronic mail than by telex, the user needs to have some fairly (expensive) equipment.
6 Documents sent by post arrive (slow) than documents sent by fax.
7 A large number of people can be reached (easy) by email.
8 My secretary understands English (good), and she can write (good) than I can, too.

13.d In the word square, find the telex abbreviations that mean the same as the words below. The words in the square may be vertical, horizontal, or diagonal, and may be read forwards or backwards.

1 Please
2 Out of order
3 Subscriber temporarily unobtainable, call the Information (Enquiry) Service
4 I shall call you back
5 Subscriber is engaged
6 Minutes
7 Repeat / I repeat
8 Error
9 Subscriber's number has been changed
10 Collation please / I collate

L	M	M	N	S	P	L	Z	S
Q	T	S	D	X	I	Y	D	A
P	F	N	I	O	X	Q	E	R
A	R	O	C	R	O	E	R	E
T	X	S	I	F	P	U	K	L
C	C	X	V	B	J	T	I	N
I	C	E	X	P	A	R	I	C
A	O	N	U	X	G	M	V	H
W	C	L	H	M	X	H	O	U

13.e Read the following five telex messages in section **A**, and match them with the replies in section **B**. The first one has been done for you.

A

1 WILL SEND SHPPG DOCS TO NATIONAL BANK GROVE STREET LONDON IMMEDIATELY +

2 CANNOT SUPPLY CAT NO 516 IN BLUE WILL BLACK BE OK + ?

3 CONSIGNMENT HELD UP SINGAPORE DUE STRIKE WILL TRY TO FIND ANOTHER VESSEL FOR SHPMNT +

4 PREPARED TO OFFER 4000 THOUSAND DOLLARS PER TON CIF NEW YORK IS THAT ACCEPTABLE 4000 DOLLARS + ?

5 ONLY ACCEPT CONSIGNMENT ORDER NO 3015 WITH 25 O/O DISC CIF HAMBURG TERMS

B

a We will accept the items that you offered us under catalogue number 516 in black. Please send the shipment by air to avoid any further delay.

b We must insist on our original quote of $4,500 per ton on ex-works prices, as the market is still rising on this exchange. And may we suggest that you accept this competitive offer.

c We can still offer a 15 per cent discount on order number 3015 on cost, insurance, freight terms with delivery to Hamburg. Could you please let us know if this is acceptable?

d Our shipbrokers have advised us that the SS Tanaku Maru, which is docked in Singapore at the moment, is available for charter. They will charge £50.00 per ton. Please telex Alliance Shipbrokers in London if these terms are acceptable.

e Thank you for the documents which arrived at the bank this morning. We are transferring $11,500 to your account 3882674 at Bank Bumiputra, Kuala Lumpur. Please send us confirmation when you have received the money.

13.f Write out the five telex messages in section **A** in ordinary English. Then write out the five replies in section **B** as telex messages.

13.g

Below are four messages that you need to send, and, in the boxes, some extra information that may possibly affect them. First, decide whether to send each message by fax, email, telex, or ordinary letter. Then write them out. You may make up addresses and fax and telex numbers if you need them.

Message 1
Harvey Watson, the manager of the Lansdown Hotel group, spent the weekend at the house of Mr Jeremy Jones, the Director of the Allied International Bank. He wants to thank Mrs Margaret Jones for her hospitality.

Message 2
The Managing Director of AA Insurance wants to inform his staff of an important change in the company. They have a new chairwoman, Mrs Susanne Durand, as from today. He feels sure that everyone will give her their full support and wants to wish her the best of luck. There haven't been any other changes in the company's personnel.

Message 3
Sally Field, of International Fashions, London, has been informed by Mr Bernard Cassard, the Manager of the Hotel Aragon in Paris, that the rooms she has booked are available and that the hotel requires a deposit of 3,500 francs for the rooms and car hire. She wants to inform him that she is sending a bank draft today for 3,500 francs as a deposit and she would like confirmation in a letter with a receipt.

Message 4
Mr Brian Newbury, of Newbury Tours, is organizing a sales conference in a week's time. He would like Paperman Promotions to supply 500 blue pens with the words 'Newbury Tours' printed on the side, as well as the company logo. This consists of an image of a flag with a crown. The logo is blue on a white background. Mr Newbury would like to know if the company can supply these, what the delivery date would be, and how much they will cost.

Information boxes
Read the following pieces of information. Remember that some of the information is important and some may not be.

Mr Cassard does not have a fax machine in his office.	The Lansdown Hotel group recently arranged a loan of £1.3 million from the Allied International Bank.
Mr Jones and Mr Watson were best friends at university.	There are more than 600 staff at AA Insurance, 200 are in London and the others are in the Cheltenham office.
Mr Newbury works in a well-equipped office with access to fax machines, computer terminals, and telexes.	Miss Field heard from Mr Cassard by telex.
Mrs Jones is a particularly good cook.	
All the staff at AA Insurance have access to computer terminals linked to a central computer.	

Miscellaneous correspondence 14

14.a Complete the following sentences by joining up the two parts with the correct preposition. The first one has been done as an example.

1	I'd be grateful if you could send them a reply . . .	FOR	relocating an office is that overheads can be reduced.
2	The main advantage . . .	TO	the closure of the factory.
4	Everyone in the bank received an invitation . . .	OF	your phone call this morning.
4	I am writing to you with reference . . .	TO	silicon chips.
5	The insurance company paid for the damage . . .	TO	the office Christmas party.
6	He was criticised by the manager . . .	OF	the stock in the fire.
7	The union leaders wanted to hear about the reasons . . .	FOR	child care facilities in the company.
8	The price of computers has gone up recently because of a shortage . . .	ON	the work you have completed.
9	I am enclosing a cheque . . .	FOR	the invitation they sent.
10	The Personnel Manager submitted the report . . .	TO	his unhelpful attitude towards the customers.

14.b Replace the incorrect preposition in each of the following sentences with the correct one.

Example
I am not very interested for new technology.
I am not very interested in new technology.

1   The Sales Manager was very disappointed from the poor sales figures.
2   The workforce at the factory are very worried on the prospect of being made redundant.
3   In our department it is the sub-manager who is responsible of checking the accounts.
4   The Director's Personal Assistant accompanied him to the Frankfurt Book Fair because she was good in German.

5   He changed job because he was fed up from doing the same things every day.
6   The agency put in extra work because they were afraid for losing the account.
7   We are very sorry of the delay, which was caused by a dock strike in Rotterdam.

14.c   Complete the following sentences about an internal transfer with the correct prepositions.

1   Madeleine has applied _____ a vacancy in the Publicity Department.

2   In her last job, she looked _____ orders and phone enquiries.

3   Now she is looking _____ something that is a bit more challenging.

4   She heard _____ the vacancy from a friend in the department.

5   She is a reliable worker who can be depended _____ to do a good job.

6   Could you let me know what you think _____ her?

7   I would like to talk _____ you about her application.

8   I think we should write _____ her soon and tell her what we have decided.

14.d   Change the following sentences into a more acceptable form for business letters.

1   I can't come to the reception because I'll be on holiday next week.

    I regret that _____

2   It's such a shame that your brother is dead. I'm really sorry.

    I was _____

3   So you've been elected Chairman of the company! Well done!

    I would like _____

4   Mr Norman wants to drop in and see you next week about a contract, OK?

    Mr Norman would _____

5   I can't see you next Friday for our appointment after all.

    I am sorry to tell _____

6   Can you come to our Sales Conference on 18 March?

    We would like _____

7   Thanks for helping me when I was in Hamburg last week.

    I would _____

8   It'll be good to see you on Friday.

    I look _____

14.e Complete the crossword.

ACROSS

1 Sales of typewriters have fallen this year because there has been much less _____ for them, but supplies have remained the same. (6)

5 In most companies the personnel officer is responsible _____ hiring new staff. (3)

6 The firm had to make several workers redundant because they had _____ many people in the factory. (3)

8 The Managing Director was not very _____ at English, so he decided to go on an intensive English course. (4)

9 Please confirm that the invoice will be paid by the _____ of this month. (3)

12 Westlake International received a number of letters enquiring _____ their new products after the advertising campaign. (5)

14 I am enclosing a cheque _____ £3,567.21. (3)

15 The management are considering the employees' _____ claim. (3)

16 Please fill in and return the reply coupon if you would be interested _____ hearing about our new range of products. (2)

18 I have not yet received a _____ _____ my letter of 18 January. (5,2)

DOWN

1 We cannot give you an exact delivery date as this will _____ on the time the vessel takes to arrive. (6)

2 Mr Volta is a reasonable manager, but he is very bad _____ communicating with his staff. (2)

3 Could you lend me a pen so that I can _____ down your fax number? (4)

5 The industrial dispute prevented the newspaper publishers _____ delivering the papers to the shops.(4)

7 See if the builders can give you a rough _____ of how much the new wing is likely to cost. (4)

10 The Marketing Manager is responsible _____ the Marketing Director, who is in overall charge of sales policy.

11 The Sales Manager had to travel to Paris by train because the air traffic controllers were on _____ . (6)

12 Mr Watson decided to _____ for the job that was advertised on the company noticeboard. (5)

13 I'm afraid that Mrs Tremain is not in the office today; she has_____ to London for a meeting. (4)

14 At the shareholders' meeting, the Chairman explained the reasons _____ the company's poor performance.

14.f Read the following invitation from the German Chamber of Commerce and the reply to it, and then choose the best words from the options in brackets.

Dear Mr Boldt,

We [1](*wish, want, would like*) to invite you to our annual dinner on 15 February and [2](*wonder, ask demanded*) if you would consider being one of our guest [3](*announcers, speakers, talkers*).

The theme we are promoting this year is the Single European Currency, and we would [4](*admire, like, appreciate*) a contribution from your field of manufacturing how this would [5](*afflict, affect, alter*) you and your colleagues' enterprises. Please [6](*let, leave, make*) us know as soon as possible if you are able to [7](*arrive, attend, assist*).

[8](*Inside, Enclosed, Within*) you will find a formal invitation [9](*to, of, for*) yourself and a guest.

Yours sincerely,

Peter Hoffman

Peter Hoffman
Chairman

Dear Mr Hoffman,

Thank you for your letter and invitation of 13 January [10](*requesting, asking, inviting*) Mr Boldt to your annual dinner.

He will be [11](*content, overjoyed, pleased*) to attend and speak about the effects that parity of currencies will have on the costs of [12](*crude, raw, first*) materials for our industry. He [13](*expects, awaits, forecasts*) the talk to last about half an hour.

I will send you a transcript next week, and Mr Boldt would [14](*enjoy, greet, welcome*) any comments or suggestions you care to [15](*have, propose, make*).

He looks forward to seeing you on February 15 at the [16](*event, occasion, function*).

Yours sincerely,

Barbara Schroeder

Barbara Schroeder (Mrs)
p.p. Gunther Boldt
Chairman

14.g Desmond Taylor, Sales Director of Data Unlimited PLC, is organizing a sales conference for forty sales representatives to attend a two-day presentation by two advertisers who are promoting a new line of products.

As Mr Taylor, write a letter to the Conference Centre based on the following information:

- Your address: Data Unlimited PLC, Data House, Chertsey Road, Twickenham, Middlesex TW1 1EP.
- Conference Centre: The Royal Hotel, Owls Road, Boscombe BH5 1AD.
- The hotel was recommended by associates and you want a conference room for forty reps for a two-day presentation.
- Dates of conference: 8 and 9 December 19—. You will need conference room and facilities from 09.00 to 18.00 on both days.
- Requirements: full seating, presentation platform, dais, public address system, screen for slides, full video equipment and facilities for recording. You will supply your own display materials.
- Refreshments: coffee/biscuits at 11.00, four-course meal in restaurant with table wine, tea/snacks at 16.00.
- Finish by asking for confirmation that the centre will be available.

14.h Two sales representatives have made a last-minute booking, but the Royal Hotel is already fully booked. Write a letter from Mr Taylor to another hotel nearby, requesting accommodation.

- The address is the Old Parsonage Hotel, 18 Forest Road, Boscombe BH6 1DA.
- The hotel was recommended by colleagues who stayed there last year.
- Two of your representatives, Mr Charles Bickford and Mrs Clare Ramal, will be coming to Boscombe and staying from 7 to 10 December inclusive.
- Ask for two single rooms with en suite facilities and half board.
- Ask the hotel to arrange the hire of a medium-sized car for this period, as the representatives will need to get to the office and the conference centre.
- Say that if they telex or fax you confirming the booking, you will immediately forward the necessary deposit to secure it.

Memorandums and reports

15

15.a Complete the following using either the present perfect continuous, (e.g. *have been working*) or the simple past, (e.g. *worked*).

---

1 Our organisation [1](*export*)_____ precision tools to the Middle East for over twenty years. We [2](*open*)_____ our first office in Iraq in the early 1960s and it [3](*remain*)_____ open for five years until we [4](*move*)_____ our headquarters to Jordan. In the last few months we [5](*negotiate*)_____ a contract with Saudi Arabia, which we hope will be signed soon.

---

2 Since the beginning of this year, the department store [6](*lose*)_____ over £3,000 per month due to theft, and last month this [7](*rise*)_____ to £6,500. We believe that a gang of shoplifters [8](*operate*)_____ in the building for the last few weeks, and that this may account for the losses that [9](*occur*)_____ in June. Over the last few days we [10](*have*)_____ discussions with our security consultants who will produce a report shortly.

---

3 Trading in the market [11](*be*) slack_____ for the first two months of the year, as investors [12](*feel*)_____ worried by the uncertain political climate, and interest rates [13](*remain*)_____ high. However in the last few weeks, interest rates [14](*fall*)_____ gradually and look as if they will continue to do so. Investors [15](*return*)_____ to the market slowly and volumes [16](*increase*)_____.

15.b   Match the sentences from column **A** with possible contexts in column **B**.

A

1   Over the past few years, the firm's profits have risen by nearly 25 per cent.
2   Over the past few years, the firm's profits have been rising by 25 per cent.
3   The company has done very well this year.
4   The company has been doing very well this year.

B

a   It is the middle of May.
b   It is the middle of December.
c   Profits rise by 25 per cent each year.
d   The total rise in profits is 25 per cent.

15.c   Read the following memo and choose the best words from the options in brackets.

NATIONAL STORES PLC
518 MARYLEBONE ROAD   LONDON W1B 3MC

To: All Staff
From: Personnel Officer
Date: 15 February 19 —
Subject: Staff discounts

We intend to introduce a staff discount [1](*project, scheme, proposal*) on February 15 for everyone working for the company.

The discount will be fifteen per cent [2](*minus, less, off*) the retail price of any [3](*objects, pieces, items*) in the store.

When purchases are [4](*made, done, bought*), staff must [5](*keep, guard, save*) receipts of anything they have bought until after exit security [6](*checks, controls, searches*) have been made. It would also be [7](*essential, important, advisable*) for staff to keep receipts for three months after purchase to [8](*demonstrate, test, prove*) when and where the item was bought.

If you have any [9](*questions, misunderstandings, enquiries*) see your manager or supervisor who will be able to help you.

15.d   The Accountant in the same department store wants to write a memo to staff about procedures for payments by cheque, and wants to remind them what steps they should take to prevent fraud. Read the following list of comments, and decide which points should be mentioned in the memo.

  a   Staff should carefully match signatures on cheque cards with signatures on cheques.
  b   The value of bad cheques presented over the past year amounts to £30,000.
  c   Salespeople should not make all the customers feel like criminals.
  d   A number of customers pay for goods in cash.
  e   Cheque cards have expiry dates and limits written on them which need to be examined carefully.
  f   Supervisors should be contacted if salespeople are unsure about a payment.
  g   Customers' reactions should be noted for nervousness.
  h   Cheques should be examined to see that they have been completed properly.
  i   The banks also lose a great deal of money through cheque fraud.
  j   The problem of bad cheques cannot be eliminated, but it can be reduced.

Write the memo and cover the following points:

■   Say what the problem is.
■   Explain what procedures staff should follow.
■   Explain what additional precautions can be taken.
■   Say what staff should do if they are still in doubt about a cheque.

15.e   The Company Secretary of Elland Hughes Advertising has been asked to prepare a report on the introduction of a flexitime system. Below are four documents that you should read and understand, before proceeding to 15.f.

Document 1   Memo to the Company Secretary

MEMO

To: Company Secretary
From: I. Peters
Subject: Flexitime

The board have recently been considering the introduction of a flexitime system. Please prepare a report on the feasibility of introducing this system. The report should cover:

1 Staff attitude towards flexitime
2 Benefits to the company of flexitime
3 Financial implications
4 Disadvantages (if any)
5 Conclusions and recommendations.

We envisage that the new times might be from 0700 to 2100, and that staff could have a day off in the week in lieu of Saturday if they prefer.

Please let me have the report and your findings by March 18.

Document 2   Staff Questionnaire

Results of Staff Questionnaire

1 Are you in favour of the introduction of a flexitime system?

YES	87%
NO	4%
DON'T KNOW	9%

2 Would you prefer to have a day off in the week instead of Saturday?

YES	76%
NO	11%
DON'T KNOW	13%

3 Which facilities do you find most crowded?

PHOTOCOPIER	35%
FAX	24%
CANTEEN	21%
PHONE	15%
TOILET	3%
OTHER	2%

4 What is your average journey time to work during the rush-hour?

LESS THAN ½ HOUR:	12%
½ HOUR TO 1 HOUR:	48%
1 HOUR TO 1½ HOURS:	29%
MORE THAN 1½ HOURS:	11%

5 If flexitime were introduced, which hours would you prefer?

7 to 3	18%
8 to 4	21%
9 to 5	16%
10 to 6	20%
11 to 7	10%
12 to 8	10%
1 pm to 9	5%

6 If the office was open six days a week, which day would you choose to have free in addition to Sunday?

Monday	16%
Tuesday	7%
Wednesday	23%
Thursday	14%
Friday	19%
Saturday	21%

7 What would be the main advantage of a free day during the week for you?

Being with partner	34%
Shopping	23%
Making other appointments	26%
Other	17%

8 In what way would the company benefit most from a flexitime system?

Overseas clients would find it easier to contact us	34%
Clients could contact us on Saturday	26%
Staff would not be tired after the rush-hour	24%
Security would be improved	12%
Other	4%

9 Would you be in favour of the introduction of a clocking-in system?

YES	26%
NO	48%
DON'T KNOW	26%

10 Would you be in favour of a one-year trial period?

YES	76%
NO	14%
DON'T KNOW	10%

Document 3   Memo from the Accounts Department

MEMO

To: Company Secretary
From: Chief Accountant
Subject: Flexitime

Your asked us to examine the financial implications of the flexitime system, and our conclusions are as follows:

Overheads will increase because of the need for extra heating and lighting. This will increase the bill by approximately 7%, but this may be offset by slightly lower insurance premiums because of the increased security of having staff on the premises longer. There may also be a reduction in photocopying costs if we do not need to use outside agencies so much. All these costs are relatively small.

Wages will not increase as long as staff who work on Saturdays do not require the overtime rate, which is the standard wage plus 50%.

The clocking-in system will cost approximately £1549 + VAT. This is a fixed cost and can be offset against tax.

A more detailed 'Costing Sheet Estimate' is attached.

Document 4   Extract from a letter to a friend

... and they're thinking of bringing in a new flexitime system, which would be marvellous for most of us. I mean, I hate shopping on Saturdays, don't you? I think I'll have Wednesdays off, because that's when John's free, so we'll be able to spend much more time together. And best of all, I'll be able to get in the morning and not face that awful rush-hour! What could be better? Lots of the other girls feel the same, and I'm sure we'll all work better in the end.

Anyway, did I tell you about ...

15.f   Based on the information you have read in 15.e, write a report from the Company Secretary, using not more than 400 words. Your report should take the following form:

- Introduction: give details of the proposed flexitime system.
- Outline the advantages to the company of the system.
- Outline the advantages to the staff of the system.
- Mention the financial costs and benefits.
- Make your conclusions and recommendations.

Personnel appointments

16

16.a Revision exercise. Choose the best answer to complete the following sentences.

1 Before we can buy the building, we need to find out who _____ it.
A do own   B is owning   C owns   D own

2 I never realised that Rolls Royce _____ engines for aeroplanes.
A made   B make   C makes   D are making

3 We'll have to send the consignment by air because the vessel _____ by the time we get it to the docks.
A will leave   B is leaving   C will have left   D is to leave

4 He says he has not received the cheque and wants to know when _____
A did we send it   B have we sent it   C we sent it   D we have sent it

5 We cannot accept cheques _____ they are guaranteed by a cheque card.
A without   B except   C only   D unless

6 The Chairman, _____ is 65 next month, will retire at the end of the year.
A that   B which   C whom   D who

7 The Manager flew to Tokyo last week _____ a joint venture agreement with Mitsubishi.
A for signing   B signing   C for to sign   D to sign

8 The equipment at the factory is working very well and we _____ any problems with it.
A haven't had   B didn't have   C hadn't   D weren't having

9 The computers we sell _____ in this country, although the parts come from Taiwan.
A assemble   B are assembling   C assembled   D are assembled

10 The management consultants have suggested _____ into Europe.
A us to expand   B us expand   C we are expanding   D we should expand

11 The Bank Manager admitted that he had _____ a mistake increasing the credit to the company.
A done   B committed   C had   D made

12 If the ship _____ delayed by bad weather, it would have arrived on time.
A wouldn't be   B wasn't   C hasn't been   D hadn't been

13 The board decided _____ the next meeting for a few weeks.
A at postponing   B to postpone   C postponing   D for postponing

14 My secretary speaks such _____ English because she spent three years in London.
A fluently   B good   C well   D better

15 I _____ to the editor since she came back from Yugoslavia.
A didn't speak   B haven't spoken   C hadn't spoken   D don't speak

16.b   Revision exercise. Complete each sentence so that it means the same as the one before it.

Example
I haven't seen our Spanish agent for three months.
The last time *I saw our Spanish agent was three months ago.*

1   We manufacture most of our computers in Korea.

Most _____

2   We didn't send the consignment by rail because there was a strike.

If there _____

3   'Do you know what the dollar rate is?' he asked me.

He asked me if _____

4   I am very sorry that I didn't reply sooner.

He apologised for _____

5   I'm afraid that the Manager will leave before you arrive.

By the time _____

6   I find these latest sales forecasts very interesting.

I am _____

7   I started working with NCR three weeks ago.

I have _____

8   My secretary is a very efficient typist.

My secretary types _____

9   'When does the sales conference finish?' the representative asked.

The representative wanted _____

10   I am not going to apply for a transfer because I haven't got the right qualifications.

I _____

16.c Complete the boxes with the missing words from the sentences below to find the 'key' word down.

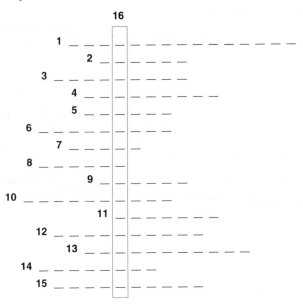

ACROSS

1 If a company offers a _____ - _____ pension scheme, they pay for your premiums.
2 Christmas Day and Easter Monday are examples of _____ holidays.
3 A prospective employer will often ask a candidate's previous employer for a _____ to find out what sort of person they are.
4 Jobs that are not temporary are _____ .
5 Free travel, subsidised food, and staff discounts are examples of _____ benefits.
6 An _____ is someone who applies for a job.
7 My current salary is £15,000 per _____ .
8 In the company we have _____ reviews of salaries every October.
9 A secretary's _____ can include typing, filing, and making appointments.
10 Successful applicants are sent a contract of _____ which sets out terms and conditions.
11 The company had a _____ for an accounts clerk, so they put an advertisement in the paper.
12 The company invited five _____ to come to the interview.
13 The _____ spent about an hour asking me questions about my previous jobs and experience.
14 She received a letter saying her application had been successful, and she was asked to sign and return the _____ giving details of the conditions of work.
15 The new cashier was introduced to all her _____ on the first day.
16 'Key' word (DOWN): The document giving details about yourself and your work history.

78

16.d Choose the best words from the options in brackets to complete the job advertisement below.

Bilingual Secretary for

INTERNATIONAL PUBLISHING LTD

60 Girton Street · Cambridge CB2 3EU

We are looking for someone with [1](*current, fluent, spoken*) English and Italian, and preferably another language, such as French or German. The [2](*secretary, interviewee, applicant*) should have at least two years' secretarial [3](*work, experience, employment*). Office skills such as typing, word processing, and shorthand would be a(n) [4](*advantage, benefit, addition*).

The work [5](*consists, contains, includes*) customer liaison, and [6](*doing, making, acting*) as an interpreter for the Assistant Manager, both here and elsewhere in Europe. The successful candidate will also be expected to proof-read manuscripts in English and Italian. In addition to this, he / she will be expected to carry out the usual secretarial [7](*work, duties, employment*).

For a(n) [8](*application form, c.v., interview*), phone Paula Prentiss, the Personnel Manager, on (0223) 6814, Ext. 412, quoting [9](*number, reference, figure*) PP 391.

16.e Read the following application form, and use it to help you write the covering letter to accompany it. You may also need to invent some of the information in the letter.

- Say what job you are applying for.
- Say why you are interested in the job, and why you would be suitable for it.

INTERNATIONAL PUBLISHING LTD
60 Girton Street · Cambridge CB2 3EU

Application form (COMPLETE IN BLOCK LETTERS)

Surname

Giuliani

Forename(s)

Carla

Address

*114 Ellesmere Walk
Finchley
London NW3 1DP*

Age

22

Date of birth

4 January 19 —

Qualifications

*Degree in English and French (Università di Genoa)
Secretarial diploma (Pitman College, London)*

Languages

*Italian (mother tongue)
French
English
German*

Office Skills

Typing (w.p.m) *60*
Shorthand (w.p.m) *85*
Wordprocessing *Yes*

Hobbies and interests

Tennis, swimming, horseriding, reading

16.f   Paula Prentiss has read Carla's application form and letter, and would like to interview her. Write the letter, inviting her to attend.

- Invite her, on behalf of the Managing Director, to come for an interview at 14.30 on 18 June, at the office. Warn her that there will be an Italian and French translation test before the interview.
- Send her a map with details, and tell her there are frequent trains to Cambridge from Liverpool Street Station.
- Ask her to phone you to confirm the date, or to arrange another one if she cannot attend.

16.g   Following a successful interview, Kevin Wheeler, the Managing Director, would like to offer Carla the post of bilingual secretary. Write his letter to her.

- Refer to the post Carla applied for and the date of her interview, and inform her that she has been accepted.
- Say when she will be expected to start.
- Send her two copies of the contract of employment, to be signed and returned to Paula Prentiss.
- Close with appropriate welcoming remarks.

Answer key

Note: For reasons of space, information such as addresses and dates is not set out at the top of most model letters in this Answer Key. If you are unfamiliar with the correct layout of a formal letter in English, you should work through the exercises in Units 1 and 2 of this Workbook before proceeding to other units.

1 Structure and presentation

1.a

1	F	Yours sincerely	9	T		
2	F	carbon copy	10	T		
3	F	Dear Mr Smith	11	F	Public Limited Company
4	F	The Chairman	12	F	Ltd.
5	T		13	T		
6	T		14	F	indented style
7	F	Dear Sir Roger, or Dear Sir Roger Dumont	15	T		
			16	F	Dr Spock
8	F	True in the USA, but in the UK, it means 6 June 1995	17	T		
			18	T		

1.b

1 is/exports
2 is having
3 is improving/are finding
4 start/go
5 is meeting/(is) doing
6 need/are negotiating
7 am writing
8 am trying/'m not having/Does he still have

1.c

1 Soundsonic Ltd., Warwick House, Warwick Street, London SE23 1JF.
2 D. Fregoni, The Chief Accountant, Fregoni S.p.A., Piazza Leonardo da Vinci 254, Milano I-20133.
3 Mr Heinz Bente, The Chairman, Bente Spedition GmbH, Feldbergstr. 30, D–6000 Frankfurt 1.
4 The Sales Manager, Sportique et cie. 201 rue Sambin, F–21000 Dijon.
5 Mrs S. Moreno, The Accountant, Intercom, 351 Avda. Luis de Morales, E–41006 Sevilla.
6 Mrs Maria Nikolakaki, Nikitara 541, 85100 Rhodes, Greece.
7 Mrs Junko Shiratori, Excel Heights 501, 7–3–8 Nakakasai, Edogawa-ku 139 Tokyo, Japan.
8 The Transport Director, VHF Vehicles Ltd., 301 Leighton Road, Kentish Town, London NW5 2QE.

1.d

1 note
2 are building
3 am writing
4 provide
5 starts
6 supply
7 are offering
8 know
9 look

1.e

1 for
2 in
3 of
4 in
5 with
6 of
7 on
8 to
9 from

1.f   Model letter:

Sender: UK Cycles Ltd., Borough House, Borough Road, Cleveland TS8 3BA
Date: 19 February 19—
Receiver: Karl Janssen, The Managing Director, Velo Sport AG, Karlstr. 45, 0–5230 Sömmerda

Dear Mr Janssen,

Thank you for your letter of 15 February, in which you asked about our terms of trade.

We give quantity discounts on orders exceeding £10,000, but cannot offer credit facilities until at least one year after beginning a business relationship. We can normally guarantee delivery of our goods within three months of receiving the order.

We have pleasure in enclosing our latest catalogue and price-list, which we hope will be of interest to you.

Thank you for your interest in UK Cycles, and we look forward to hearing from you.

Yours sincerely,

Robert Morris
Sales Director

Enc.

2 Content and style

2.a

1 will be met	7 will need
2 will be staying	8 will not be able
3 leave	9 will be visiting
4 will travel	10 will have returned
5 will have had	11 suit
6 arrive	

2.b   Dear Sir/Madam

We saw a large selection of your products at the Frankfurt Fair, which was held last June, and may be interested in retailing them through our outlets in Germany.

We are particularly interested in your industrial ware, including overalls, boots, helmets, gloves, and fire-proof jackets. Could you send us your latest catalogue and price-list, quoting c.i.f. terms to Hamburg.

We can assure you that if your prices and discounts are competitive, we will place regular, large orders. We look forward to hearing from you soon.

Yours faithfully,

T. Hamacher
Chief Buyer

2.c   Model letter:

Dear Sir,

We are writing concerning the February balance of £567.00, which has been outstanding for three months. We wrote to you on the 15 March and 4 April asking you to clear this account, but did not receive a reply, which surprised us as you have been regular customers of ours for a number of years.

We would like to remind you that credit was offered on the understanding that balances would be cleared on the due dates; failure to do so could create difficulties for us with our own suppliers.

We are prepared to offer you a further ten days to clear this account, or explain why you cannot do so, otherwise we will, reluctantly, have to take legal action.

Yours faithfully,

R. Lancaster

2.d   Model memo:

We've had a letter from T.D. Games, apologizing for not settling his account. This was due to a serious fire in his plant, which destroyed the company's records. However, the company's insurers are about to release funds to enable them to start settling their debts, and Mr Games assures us that we will be repaid fully in due course. Meanwhile, he has enclosed a cheque for £55.00.

2.e   Model letter:

> Sarah Barnard,
> Barnard Press Ltd
> 183–7 Copwood Road
> London N12 9PR
>
> J. Bini   2 March 19 —
> International Books
> Via Santovetti 117/9
> 00045 Grottaferrata
> Roma
>
> Our Ref: RW/SB
>
> Dear Mr Bini,
>
> Thank you for your enquiry of 15 February about story-books in English and Italian for students of an intermediate level.
>
> We are sorry to say that these books are not in stock at present, but we are in the process of publishing a new series for the summer, and I am enclosing a list which you might be interested in, together with our current catalogue.
>
> Yours sincerely,
>
>
> p.p. Sarah Barnard
> Managing Director
>
> Encl.

3   Enquiries

3.a
1 —	6 the	11 —	16 —
2 the	7 a	12 —	17 the
3 The	8 a	13 —	18 a
4 the	9 the	14 the	19 the
5 the	10 the	15 a	

3.b   a 4   b 2   c 5   d 6   e 3   f 1

3.c
1   I would be grateful for a copy of your latest brochure.
2   Could you please tell us how much discount you will give on orders of 5,000 units?
3   I am writing to enquire when we can expect to receive the cheque.
4   Please let us know if you would like us to arrange an appointment with one of our representatives.
5   Do you happen to know if Mr Crane has returned from the Menswear Exhibition yet?
6   Could you tell us if your company exports to South Korea?

3.d
1 subsidiary (f)	3 showroom (d)	5 estimate (c)	7 prospectus (h)
2 customer (g)	4 catalogue (a)	6 tender (e)	8 wholesaler (b)

3.e   Model answers:
1   We would be grateful for details of prices.
2   I am afraid we are out of stock at the moment. We would advise you to contact us again in two weeks' time.
3   We would like delivery of the items in three months.
4   Please send us your catalogue and price-list.
5   Could you let us know what your terms of trade are?
6   If you are unable to deliver the goods before Friday, please contact us.
7   Would it be possible for you to send someone here to give us an estimate?
8   We would be grateful if we could have twenty units on approval.

3.f
1 at	3 in	5 from	7 to	9 of/about	11 in
2 of	4 in	6 for	8 by	10 for	12 with

3.g   Model letter:

Dear Sir/Madam,

I am planning a business trip to Frankfurt for myself and two colleagues, and would like details of flights and hotel tariffs during the month of March. Would it be necessary also to pay a deposit on the booking?

In addition to the flights and hotel, we intend to hire a car for two days. Please could you send details of hire rates and conditions.

Thank you for your attention, and I would be grateful for a reply at your earliest convenience.

Yours faithfully,

Carol Ross

3.h

1	retailing	5	regret
2	response	6	current
3	established	7	selection
4	terms	8	highly

3.i Model letter:

Sender: J. F. Morreau, 1150 bvd. Dalbert, F–54015 Nancy Cedex
Date: 7 July 19—
Receiver: J. Merton, Glaston Potteries Ltd., Clayfield, Burnley BB10 1RQ

Dear Mr Merton

I was impressed by your Willow Pattern dinner sets, advertised in the May edition of *International Homes*, and may be interested in retailing a selection from your range through our outlets in France.

It might be useful if I give you some idea of the terms we usually deal on. As a rule we get a 20 per cent trade discount off ex-works prices, and a 10 per cent quantity discount if we place orders of over £8,000. We would expect delivery within two months of placing an order, and would settle by 60-day bill of exchange.

Please send us a catalogue and price-list. I look forward to hearing from you soon.

Yours sincerely

Jean Morreau

4 Replies and quotations

4.a 1, 2, 3, 4, 6, 7, 9, 11

4.b
1 He asked how soon the goods could be delivered.
2 He asked for details of their prices.
3 He wanted to know where the goods could be purchased.
4 He asked if there was an after-sales service.
5 He asked how long the goods were guaranteed for.
6 He wanted to know what their terms of payment were.
7 He asked if they gave quantity discounts, and if so, how much they were.
8 He wondered if they could send details of the range of goods available.

4.c

1	enquiry	5	outlets	9	quantity
2	products	6	catalogue	10	bill
3	trade	7	samples	11	wide
4	label	8	c.i.f.		

4.d

1	discussing, to say, to delay	4	enclosing
2	asking	5	retailing, receiving
3	to make	6	promoting, to launch

4.e

1	by	3	at	5	in	7	in	9	for	11	in	13	to
2	of	4	in	6	of	8	of	10	of	12	of		

4.f   Model letter:

Sender: Busch AG, Leopoldstr. 501, D–8000 München 3
Date: 18 June 19—
Receiver: The Sales Director, GDM Ltd., 516 Gipsy Rd., Headington, Oxford OX3 OBP

Dear Miss Croft

Thank you for your letter of 10 June, enquiring about our range of office furniture. I am enclosing a catalogue and price-list, quoting c.i.f. terms London.

Our products are manufactured using the highest quality materials, and all are guaranteed for two years. We are not able to offer credit terms as our profit margins are small due to our highly competitive prices. However, we can offer a discount of three per cent for a cash settlement.

Once again, thank you for your interest in our company, and do not hesitate to contact us if there is any further information you require.

Yours sincerely

Birgit Lange
p.p. Gerd Busch
Sales Director

Enc.

5 Orders

5.a

1	consignment	6	alternative
2	wrapped	7	delivery
3	packed	8	settle
4	crates	9	hand over
5	depot	10	transaction

5.b

1	d	arrives/will (shall) have to
2	a	will (shall) be able/order
3	e	are wrapped/get
4	c	are/will accept
5	f	will send/are
6	b	is/will (shall) place

5.c

1 Unless we hear from you, we'll assume there are no problems.
2 If your order was (were) larger, we would be able to give you a fifteen per cent discount.
3 As soon as we receive your order, we'll despatch the goods immediately.
4 Provided that we receive the necessary documents within fourteen days, we will process your order.
5 If we do not have the colour you require in stock, would you accept an alternative?
6 Unless you supply a letter of credit, we cannot accept your order.

5.d

1	place	3	deliver	5	confirm	7	refuse
2	cancel	4	despatched	6	shipped	8	made up

5.e

1	concerning	3	apologize	5	taken on	7	care	9	according
2	placed	4	shortage	6	reach	8	consignment	10	prevent

5.f

Quantity	Item description	Cat No.	Price c.i.f.	Total
50	Plain white shirts	S298	30	1,500
50	Plain blue shirts	S288	30	1,500
20	Plain red pullovers	P112	40	800
20	Plain blue pullovers	P155	40	800

Amount due: ___DM 4,600_____

Terms of payment: ___banker's draft_____

Requested delivery date: ___16 June 19 —_____

5.g Model letter:

Sender: Reiner GmbH, Wessumer Strasse 215–18, D–4500 Osnabrück
Date: 5 May 19—
Receiver: D. Causio, Satex S.p.A., Via di Pietra Papa, 00146 Roma

Dear Mr Causio

Thank you for your letter of 1 May, enclosing your current catalogue and price-list.

Please find enclosed my order. As we agreed, settlement will be by banker's draft, when we receive the shipping documents, and we expect delivery within six weeks.

If the items requested are not available, please do not send substitutes.

We would be grateful if you could inform us at once if there are any problems with delivery.

We look forward to receiving acknowledgement of our order at your earliest possible convenience.

Yours sincerely

Sabine Muss
p.p. D. Faust
Buying Manager

5.h Model letter:

Sender: Yacht Internationale, 12 bvd. Salvador, F–13006 Marseille.
Date: 25 September 19—
Receiver: Mr H. Kjaer, Sales Director, Dansk Industries, Kongens Nytorv 1, DK-København K.

Dear Mr Kjaer

Please find enclosed our order (R497) for a consignment of navigational instruments.

As we agreed, the goods should be packed individually in eight crates, all numbered, and with our logo visible. Please send the instruments air freight, c.i.f. Marseille, to reach us no later than 18 May.

Please itemize all individual costs, and the trade and quantity discounts of 12 and 3 per cent respectively, on the invoice. This should be forwarded, along with the insurance certificate and Air Waybill, to The Bank of Marseille, 153–6 avenue Charles de Gaulle, F–12019 Marseille, where we will hand over our sight draft.

We look forward to receiving your consignment.

Yours sincerely

Anne Lenoir
p.p. Jacques Delmas

6 Payment

6.a 1 in which 2 which, which 3 who, which 4 —/which/that 5 which

6.b 1 to cash 3 explaining 5 to find out 7 to settle
2 giving 4 to ask 6 to recover

6.c 1 promissory 4 order 7 giro
2 refund 5 draft 8 proforma
3 invoice 6 demand 9 transfer

6.d 1 a 2 b 3 c 4 a 5 c 6 a

6.e Model letter:

Thank you for your payment of £550, which we received on the 9th May. We would however like to remind you that your account still has an outstanding balance of £2,000 in respect of other orders to date.

We should be grateful for settlement of this before the end of June. Since we began trading, you have always settled on the due dates. Therefore, if there are any problems which I may be able to help you with, please do not hesitate to call me personally and we can discuss it further. It may be possible to make alternative arrangements for settling/clearing your account.

6.f 1 account 3 clear 5 offer 7 account
2 for 4 on 6 with 8 within

6.g Model letter:

Sender: Velosport AG, Karlstr. 45, 0–5230 Sömmerda
Date: 2 June 19—
Receiver: The Accountant, UK Cycles Ltd, Borough House, Borough Road,
Cleveland TS1 3BA

Dear Mrs Stuart

Thank you for your letters of 19 March and 28 April, regarding our delay in settling our account with you.

Unfortunately, a recent fire at our Head Office has destroyed a great deal of our computer data, with the result that all correspondence, with both suppliers and customers, has been disrupted. I am afraid that it will take a while before we can return to a normal routine.

Would it be possible for you to allow us a further 30 days to clear our account? By this time, our insurance company will have released their funds, and the outstanding amount can be paid to you in full.

I would be most grateful if you could assist in this matter.

Yours sincerely

Karl Janssen
Managing Director

6.h

Quantity	Description	Cat. No.	£ each	£
10	Lotus pattern	L305	£35,00	£350,00
20	Wedgewood	W218	£43,00	£860,00
		Total	£ 1,210,00	
		Less		%
	Payment due:		£ 1,028,50	
	Signed:			

6.i   Model letter:

Sender: Glaston Potteries Ltd., Clayfield, Burnley BB10 1RQ
Date: 9 May 19—
Receiver: J. F. Morreau, 1150 bvd. Dalbert, F–54015 Nancy Cedex

Dear Mr Morreau,

Please find enclosed our invoice No. 2087/A5, for £1,210.00. The trade discount of 15 per cent, which we agreed on, brings the total payment due to £1,028.50. Prices quoted include c.i.f. Nancy.

As we discussed, payment should be made to us by sight draft, and we will ensure delivery to you within two months.

Thank you for your order.

Yours sincerely,

J. Merton
Enc.

7   Complaints and adjustments

7.a

1 received		6 showed	
2 were damaged		7 have not arrived	
3 unpacked		8 have not had	
4 found		9 have informed	
5 was torn		10 have contacted	

7.b

1 did not have, have already received
2 have had, lost, have not found
3 have looked, was
4 received, ordered
5 was, have now put

6 have recently found, manufactured
7 received, have credited
8 has informed, have not yet received, sent
9 have not had, made
10 have lost, started

7.c   1 b 2 b 3 a 4 b
All words in 5 and 6 are spelled correctly, but note that 5a and 6a are American spellings.

7.d   1 b 2 i 3 j 4 a 5 d 6 e 7 g 8 f 9 c 10 h

7.e   Model letter:

Sender: Seymore Furniture Ltd., Tib Street, Maidenhead, Berks SL6 5DS
Date: 20 October 19—
Receiver: The Managing Director, C.R. Méndez S.A., Avda. del Ejército 83, E–48015 Bilbao

Dear Mr Méndez,

Invoice no. G3190/1

Thank you for your letter of 15 October, informing us about the damage to our consignment of garden furniture. I would like to apologize for the inconvenience caused.

The goods left our warehouse in perfect condition, and therefore any damage must have occurred during transit. I shall be contacting the transport company immediately to arrange compensation.

The goods will be accepted carriage forward, and you will be refunded by banker's draft as soon as they reach us.

Once again, let me say how sorry I am that this consignment was not up to our usual high standards, and I assure you that this will not be repeated.

Yours sincerely,

M. Harrison
Sales Manager

7.f   1 Had we known they were going out of business, we would not have given them credit.
2 In our letter of 5 January, we complained about poor workmanship.
3 An error has been made in your September statement.
4 The secretary told me to contact their accounts department.
5 Could you return the consignment, before we give you a refund.
6 The problem will be dealt with as soon as we have the details.
7 The credit is so large that we cannot allow it.
8 Not only did they offer to exchange the goods, but they also gave us a discount.
9 After you have filled out the details on the credit application form, please return it to us.

7.g
1 the	5 —	9 an
2 a	6 the	10 the
3 the	7 —	
4 the	8 a	

7.h Model letter:

Sender: Nihon Instruments, 12–18 Wakakusa-cho, Higashi-Osaka-Shi, Osaka-fu
Date: 25 June 19—
Receiver: Carlo Lotti, Istituto di Medicina, Viale Bracci, I–61001 Siena

Dear Mr Lotti,

Consignment no. AWB 4156/82

Thank you for your letter of 15 June, in which you pointed out a late delivery on the above consignment.

We certainly understand how important prompt deliveries are to the institutions that use our products. However, the two orders you mentioned were sent to our factory, which delayed forwarding.

We should like to remind you that all correspondence should be sent to our administrative offices at the above address. We realize that Japanese addresses may cause some difficulties, and are therefore enclosing a supply of address labels which you can affix to all your correspondence with us.

We hope this will be helpful, and look forward to continued good trading with you.

Yours sincerely,

Hirio Toda
Sales Manager
Encl.

8 Credit

8.a

1	have been trading	5	would be settled
2	have been cleared	6	has passed
3	began	7	place
4	had been established	8	may be approached

8.b

1 Credit facilities can only be granted if a customer can satisfy a number of requirements.
2 We would like to confirm that settlement will be made against monthly statements.
3 We cannot offer open account terms, as our products are priced very competitively.
4 The enclosed invoice will be included on your next statement.
5 Our bank have advised us that the proceeds of our letter of credit have been credited to your account.
6 We have found that this firm has had to be reminded several times to settle their accounts.
7 Would you please tell us if court action has ever been taken against this firm?
8 Our investigation into Falcon Retailers has now been completed.
9 An action was brought against the firm by LDM Ltd. in 1979.
10 Could you tell us whether they can be relied on to settle their accounts promptly?

8.c

1	promptly	5	overdue
2	sufficient, elapsed, settle	6	acceptable
3	request	7	competitive
4	confidential		

8.d

1	to	3	of	5	of	7	on/by	9	for
2	on	4	at	6	for	8	up	10	at

8.e

1	credit-worthiness	3	limit	5	due	7	information
2	customer	4	balances	6	statements	8	confidence

8.f   Model letter:

Sender: Antonio Medina S.L., C/Sagasta 1156, Barcelona 08317
Date: 7 June 19—
Receiver: David Arnold, Accountant, D.L. Cromer Ltd., Central Trading Estate,
        Staines, Middx. TW18 4UP

Dear Mr Arnold

We are pleased to be able to inform you that your request for new payment terms has been accepted, and that they will come into effect as of when you place your next order with us.

We look forward to hearing from you.

Yours sincerely

P. Gómez
Sales Manager

9   Banking

9.a

1	suggest	3	advise	5	admit	7	apologize
2	refuse	4	promise	6	explain		

9.b

1 (She) suggested that (I) think it over for a few days.
2 (She) refused to extend (my) overdraft.
3 (She) advised us to consider (their) terms before making a decision.
4 (She) promised to let (me) have the details the next day.
5 (She) admitted to making a mistake on (my) October statement.
6 (She) explained that the bank would want about 120% in securities to cover the credit.
7 (She) apologized for the delay in replying to (my) request.

9.c

1	acting	4	valid	7	draw
2	inform	5	charges	8	settle
3	opened	6	documents		

9.d   Model answers:

1 Please repay the credit within the next ten days.
2 Could you send us an application form?
3 We should like to know what the rate of interest is.
4 We should like credit for a six-month period.
5 Could you tell us when we would be expected to repay the loan?
6 We would like to close our account with you.

9.e

1	completing	6	confirmation
2	payable	7	reference
3	insurance	8	arrangement
4	overdraft	9	signature
5	receipt	10	expansion

9.f   Model memo:

I had a meeting with a customer, Richard Grey, on 17 September. He admitted that his company had had difficulties recently, but he would like to expand his fleet of lorries, by buying a further two second-hand vehicles, and has requested an extension on his loan to cover the investment.

I informed Mr Grey that we would have to refuse an extension on his existing loan, but that we may be able to offer a bridging loan. He would need around £30,000 to purchase the lorries, but he is confident that the extra revenue generated by a bigger fleet would enable him to repay us within a year. He is able only to offer the lorries themselves as security for the loan.

9.g   Model letter:

Sender: The Counties Bank, 60 City Road, Salford M5 4WT
Date: 15 July 19—
Receiver: Richard Grey, Grey Transport Ltd., 350 Dock Street, Salford M6 3WT

Dear Mr Grey

Further to our meeting on 2 July, I am sorry to inform you that we will not be able to offer you a bridging loan at the present time.

Our decision to turn down your request was influenced by the current economic recession, which has affected our policy on loans to all sectors of industry and commerce. Furthermore, our directors now insist that all loans should be covered by negotiable securities, such as shares or bonds.

You may, however, be able to raise the capital you need from other sources, such as finance houses. Nevertheless, I should warn you that such sources will probably charge a higher rate of interest than that levied by us.

Once again, I am sorry not to have better news for you, but hope that we may be of more help in the future.

Yours sincerely

John Steele
Manager

10   Agents and agencies

10.a

1	do	6	do	11	did	16	make
2	do	7	do	12	did	17	do
3	made	8	make	13	made		
4	makes	9	do	14	made		
5	made	10	made	15	doing		

10.b

```
                    12
        1 S T O │C│ K B R O K E R
          2    C│O│ N F I R M I N G
    3 S O L E A G│E│N T
        4 C O M M│I│S S I O N
        5 P R I N│C│I P A L
  6 F A C T O R I│N│G
              7 │N│E T
          8 C O M│M│O D I T Y
      9 D E L C R│E│D E R E
          10    │O│W N A C C O U N T
      11 M A R K E│T│
```

10.c

1 make...up	3 do without	5 back...up	7 take on	9 fill in
2 make...out	4 taken over	6 turn down	8 work out	10 cut off

10.d

1 said	3 sole	5 trial	7 offer	9 researchers
2 approval	4 settle	6 extend	8 cost	10 current

10.e

1 c   2 a   3 c   4 c   5 c   6 a

10.f

1 recommendation	4 principals	7 rates	10 del credere
2 manufacturers	5 freight	8 documentation	11 offer
3 terms	6 factory	9 commission	12 brochure

10.g

Model letter:

Sender: Portuguese Industrial Importers, Rua dos Santos 179, 1200 Lisboa
Date: 3 July 19—
Receiver: The Managing Director, The Kobelt Agency, Braunegger Str. 618, D–4400 Münster

Dear Mr Kobelt

Thank you for your letter of 24 June in which you expressed an interest in being a buying agent for us in Germany.

We are interested in your proposals owing to an increasing demand for precision tools in Portugal. However, we would need further details of your terms before we make a final decision.

We would be prepared to accept a 3% commission on c.i.f. values, or the del credere commission you offered of 2.5%. We would also like to know whether you can act as clearing or forwarding agents, with a door-to-door facility.

It is our policy to ask for references from two other companies that you act for, so please send us details of the people that we can approach.

If possible, we should like to arrange a meeting in the near future with one of your directors, in order to discuss a contract, and clarify any outstanding matters.

I look forward to hearing from you at your earliest convenience.

Yours sincerely

Cristina Neves
Buying Manager

11 Transportation

1	when	3	in case	5	when	7	when
2	unless	4	unless	6	If		

11.b

1 If the goods had been insured, the firm would have received compensation.
2 If the dockers hadn't been on strike, the shipment wouldn't have arrived late.
3 The goods wouldn't have arrived late if the company had sent the shipment by rail.
4 If the goods had been perishable, they wouldn't have been sent by rail.
5 The consignor would have received compensation if the carriers had been negligent.
6 If we'd used our normal forwarding agents, these problems wouldn't have arisen.
7 If the records and tapes had been packed properly, they wouldn't have been damaged.

11.c

1	clearing agent (j)	6	consignee (f)	11	crates (k)
2	perishable goods (m)	7	fragile (l)	12	Baltic Exchange (h)
3	dirty (b)	8	container vessels (a)	13	bill of lading (c)
4	waybill (d)	9	certificate of origin (n)	14	dock receipt (g)
5	negligence (i)	10	freight account (e)		

11.d

1	to	3	with	5	in	7	of	9	to	11	by	13	of
2	by	4	for	6	of	8	of	10	in	12	on	14	in

11.e

Thank you for your letter of 10 November, in which you asked about charges for the transportation of your goods in Europe.

We are enclosing our tariff list, which includes all transport, customs, and documentation charges for shipments.

We can certainly promise safe transport, as we have a lot of experience in handling products for manufacturers.

If you have any further enquiries, we will be pleased to help you.

Meanwhile, should you decide to use Dietmann Spedition for your consignment to Switzerland, please return the enclosed 'Freight Forwarding Instructions Form'.

11.f

Model fax:

Dear Sir/Madam,

We are interested in using National Containers Ltd. to transport and deliver, door-to-door, a number of consignments in Europe over the next few months.

Our consignments consist of fragile crockery. An average crate measures 187 × 172 × 165 cm, and weighs approximately 35kg.

Could you please send a quotation and details of schedules. I would also be grateful for information about the necessary documentation.

Yours faithfully,

J. Merton
Sales Manager

11.g

1	above	6	suggest	11	responsibilities
2	full	7	on	12	basis
3	schedules	8	handed	13	if
4	reach	9	depot		
5	documentation	10	charged		

12 Insurance

12.a

1	getting, to go	5	to pay, to have
2	getting, losing	6	to meet, to read
3	to afford, to ask	7	to arrange, to export (exporting)
4	to want, to avoid, paying	8	to send, hearing

12.b   1 e   2 c   3 a   4 f   5 d   6 b

12.c

1	insurance	4	insured	7	proposal
2	syndicates	5	premium	8	claims
3	policy	6	Lloyd's	9	fidelity

12.d

1	large	6	supply	11	competitive
2	dealing	7	covering	12	consider
3	which	8	include	13	soon
4	to	9	kind		
5	would like	10	premises		

12.e

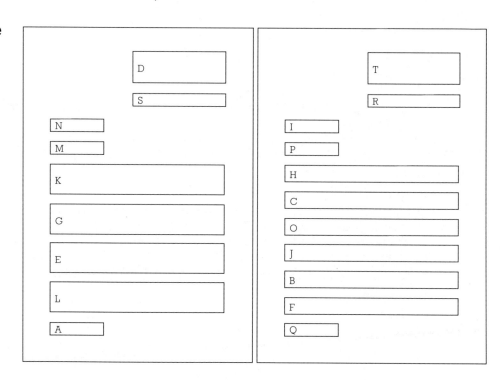

12.f 1 with   3 in   5 on   7 on
       2 for   4 to   6 under   8 of

12.g Model letter:

Sender: Sugden and Able, Insurance Brokers, 63 Grover Street, Manchester M5 6LD
Date: 4 May 19—
Receiver: UK Engineering PLC, Brunel House, Brunel Street, Liverpool L2 2ER

Dear Mr Turner

Thank you for your letter of May 1, in which you enquired about insurance cover for your shipments of machine parts.

You are correct to assume that it is expensive to insure individual shipments, and that there are policies available which cover all shipments during a period of time.

Insurance underwriters offer two types of policy which would be suitable for your requirements.

1 A floating policy, which will cover all shipments with a maximum amount, and which can be renewed when necessary.

2 An open cover policy, in which the shipper informs the underwriter when the shipment is made, and renews the policy after shipment.

I enclose a proposal form, and would be grateful if you could complete it and return it to me with details of your shipments and destinations, so that we can contact the underwriters for a premium quotation, which, I assure you, will be very competitive.

Please contact us if you require any further information.

Yours sincerely

p.p. A. Able
Director
Enc.

12.h Model letter:

Sender: Humbolt Exporters Ltd., Exode House, 115 Tremona Road, Southampton
          SO9 4XY
Date: 14 July 19—
Receiver: International Insurance PLC, 153 Western Road, Brighton, Sussex

Dear Sir,

Policy No. 439178/D

We would like to inform you that fire broke out in our warehouse on 8 July 19—, owing to an electrical fault in the building. The blaze was dealt with quickly by the Fire Service, but damage was sustained to a quantity of textiles stored there, ready for shipment. The approximate value of the damaged goods amounts to £7,000.

I would be grateful if you could send me the necessary insurance claims forms.

Yours faithfully,

Peter Hind
Company Secretary

13 Electronic correspondence

13.b

1 abbreviations	5 numerous	9 convert
2 further	6 accurately	10 password
3 similar	7 transmitted	
4 subscriber	8 requires	

13.c

1 I've just received the longest fax I've ever had in my life.
2 In certain developing countries, telexes are more reliable than faxes.
3 She couldn't read the fax very well, so she asked them to send another copy immediately, and the second one was much better.
4 Our latest telex machine is one of the most efficient available, and it is also cheaper than our competitors'.
5 Although some messages can be sent more efficiently by electronic mail than by telex, the user needs to have some fairly expensive equipment.
6 Documents sent by post arrive more slowly than documents sent by fax.
7 A large number of people can be reached easily by email.
8 My secretary understands English well, and she can write better than I can, too.

13.d

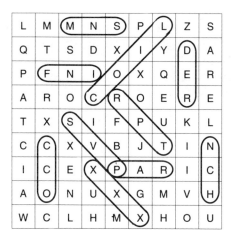

13.e

1 e	2 a	3 d	4 b	5 c

13.f

1 We will send the shipping documents to National Bank, Grove Street, London, immediately.
2 We cannot supply catalogue number 516 in blue. Will black be all right? Please reply.
3 The consignment has been held up in Singapore due to a strike. We will try to find another vessel for shipment.
4 We are prepared to offer four thousand dollars per ton, c.i.f. New York. Is that acceptable? Please reply.
5 We can only accept consignment order No. 3015 with a 25% discount c.i.f. Hamburg. Please reply.

a CAT NO 516 IN BLACK ACCEPTABLE SHIP BY AIR AVOIDING DELAY 516 BLACK +

b QUOTE £4500 FOUR THOUSAND FIVE HUNDRED STERLING PER TON EXWORKS STANDS MARKET RISING SUGGEST YOU ACCEPT £4500 EXWORKS + ?

c 15 0/0 DISC ORDER NO 315 HAMBURG STANDS ACCEPTABLE 15 0/0 CIF HAMBURG +?

d SHIPBROKERS ADVISE SS TANAKU MARU DOCKED SINGAPORE AVAILABLE FOR CHARTER QUOTE £5000 FIVE THOUSAND STERLING PER TON PLS TELEX ALLIANCE SHIPBROKERS LONDON IF ACCEPTABLE +

e TNKS FOR DOCS ARRIVED BANK THIS MORNING WILL TRANSFER $11,000 TO YR ACC NO 3882674 BANK BUMIPUTRA KUALA LUMPUR +?

13.g Model answers:

Message 1 (ordinary letter)

Dear Margaret,

I'd like to thank you for giving me such a warm welcome at your home last weekend. It was nice to see you again after all this time. I really must compliment you on the wonderful food you prepared – I hope it wasn't too much trouble.

Naturally, Mary and I would love to have the opportunity of returning your kind hospitality. So if you fancy a weekend in the country sometime, just give us a call!

Best wishes,

Harvey

Message 2 (email message)

TO: All Staff
FROM: The Managing Director
POSTED: 16 July 19—   10.46
SUBJECT:
Appointment of Mrs Susanne Durand as Chairwoman. We are pleased to announce the election of Mrs Susanne Durand as Chairwoman of AA Insurance Services as from 27 July. I know we will give her our full support and we wish her every success in this important position.
Apart from Mrs Durand's appointment, there are no other changes in the company with regard to personnel, positions, or conditions.

Message 3 (telex)

REMITTING DEPOSIT 3500 FF THREE THOUSAND FIVE HUNDRED FRENCH FRANCS BY BANK DRAFT RE BKG S FIELD PLUS CAR HIRE SEND CNFMG LETTER PLUS RECEIPT
RMTG 3500 FF BANK DRAFT 10 0/0 DPST +
INTERFASH LONDON

Message 4 (fax)

ATTN. J. NORMAN
PAPERMAN PROMOTIONS FAX 0237 889868
No. OF PAGES   1

John

We're organizing a sales conference next week, and I wonder if you could supply us 500 promotional pens with the words 'Newbury Tours' printed on the side, as well as the company logo. I'm sending the logo design separately by post.

If you can manage this, please let me know details of when you could deliver, and how much the order will cost.

Thanks.

Brian

14 Miscellaneous correspondence

14.a

2 The main advantage of relocating an office is that overheads can be reduced.
3 Everyone in the bank received an invitation to the office Christmas party.
4 I am writing to you with reference to your phone call this morning.
5 The insurance company paid for the damage to the stock in the fire.
6 He was criticized by the manager for his unhelpful attitude towards the customers.
7 The union leaders wanted to hear about the reasons for the closure of the factory.
8 The price of computers has gone up recently because of a shortage of silicon chips.
9 I am enclosing a cheque for the work you have completed.

14.b

1 The Sales Manager was very disappointed with (by) the poor sales figures.
2 The workforce at the factory are very worried (at) by the prospect of being made redundant.
3 In our department it is the sub-manager who is responsible for checking the accounts.
4 The Director's Personal Assistant accompanied him to the Frankfurt Book Fair because she was good at German.
5 He changed job because he was fed up with (of) doing the same things every day.
6 The agency put in extra work because they were afraid of losing the account.
7 We are very sorry for the delay, which was caused by a dock strike in Rotterdam.

14.c

1 for	3 for	5 on	7 to
2 after	4 about (of)	6 of	8 to

14.d

1 I regret that I shall be unable to attend the reception next week due to my holiday commitments.
2 I was most sorry to hear that your brother has died.
3 I would like to congratulate you on your election as Chairman of the company.
4 Mr Norman would like to arrange a meeting next week, in order to discuss a contract.
5 I am sorry to tell you that I will be unable to attend our appointment next Friday, after all.
6 We would like to know if you will be able to attend our Sales Conference on 18 March.
7 I would like to thank you for your help when I was in Hamburg last week.
8 I look forward to seeing you on Friday.

14.e

1 D	E	M	2 A	3 N	4 D	■	5 F	O	R
E	■	■	6 T	O	O	■	R	■	■
P	■	7 I	■	T	■	8 G	O	O	D
9 E	N	D	■	E	■	■	M	■	■
N	■	E	■	■	■	10 T	■	11 S	■
D	■	A	■	12 A	B	O	U	T	■
■	13 G	■	■	P	■	■	■	R	■
14 F	O	R	■	15 P	A	Y	■	16 I	N
17 O	N	■	■	L	■	■	■	K	■
18 R	E	P	L	Y	T	O	■	E	■

14.f

1 would like
2 wondered
3 speakers
4 like
5 affect
6 let
7 attend
8 Enclosed
9 for
10 inviting
11 pleased
12 raw
13 expects
14 welcome
15 make
16 function

14.g

Model letter:

Sender: Data Unlimited PLC, Data House, Chertsey Road, Twickenham, Middx. TW1 1EP
Date: 17 May 19—
Receiver: Reservations, The Royal Hotel, Owls Road, Boscombe BH5 1AD

Dear Sir/Madam

We are holding a conference in Boscombe this year, and your hotel was recommended to us by our associates. We should like to reserve accommodation and conference facilities for forty sales representatives, who will be attending a two-day presentation by advertisers.

The conference is scheduled to take place on the 8 and 9 December of this year, and we would require a conference room and facilities from 09.00 to 18.00 on both days.

We would need the following facilities: full seating, presentation platform, dais, public address system, screen for slides, full video equipment, and recording facilities. We will supply our own visual display materials.

We should like coffee and biscuits to be served at 11.00, a four-course lunch in the restaurant including table wine, and tea and snacks to be served at 16.00.

Please provide confirmation of our booking as soon as possible.

Yours faithfully

Desmond Taylor
Sales Director

14.h Model letter:

Sender: Data Unlimited PLC, Data House, Chertsey Road, Twickenham, Middx.
     TW1 1EP
Date: 18 November 19—
Receiver: The Old Parsonage Hotel, 18 Forest Road, Boscombe BH6 1DA

Dear Sir/Madam

Your hotel was recommended to me by three of my colleagues, who stayed there last year.

I should like to book accommodation for two of our sales representatives, Mr Charles Bickford and Mrs Clare Ramal, for three nights, from 7 to 10 December.

My colleagues require half board accommodation in two single rooms with en suite facilities.

Would it also be possible for you to arrange car hire for this period, to enable the representatives to reach the office and the conference centre at the Royal Hotel. A medium-sized car would be adequate.

Please confirm the booking, either by telex or fax, and I will forward the necessary deposit to secure it.

Yours faithfully

Desmond Taylor

15 Memorandums and reports

15.a
1 has been exporting	7 rose	13 remained
2 opened	8 has been operating	14 have been falling
3 remained	9 occurred	15 have been returning
4 moved	10 have been having	16 have been increasing
5 have been negotiating	11 was	
6 has been losing	12 felt	

15.b 1 d   2 c   3 b   4 a

15.c
1 scheme	4 made	7 advisable
2 off	5 keep	8 prove
3 items	6 checks	9 questions

15.d   Possible answers: a   b   e   f   h   j

Model memo:

TO: All Staff
FROM: Accounts Department
SUBJECT: Payments by cheque in the Store

Staff should be aware that fraud is on the increase; bad cheques presented in this store over the past year amounted to £30,000, and it is important for all salespeople to be extremely vigilant.

There are a number of procedures which should be followed in order to help minimize fraud:

1 Signatures on cheque cards and cheques should be matched carefully, and expiry dates and limits on cards should be checked.
2 You must make sure that cheques have been completed properly.
3 If you are unsure about a payment, contact a supervisor immediately.

Following the above procedures is not going to eliminate the problem of bad cheques, but we can reduce the number which get through.

15.f   Model report:

TO: All Staff
FROM: The Company Secretary

Report on the proposed new flexitime system

We have now completed our research into the proposed change to a new flexitime system for all personnel. Under the new system, employees would select their preferred working hours from 07.00 to 21.00, Monday to Saturday. They would work their normal eight-hour periods, with a one-hour lunch break. A questionnaire has been circulated to all interested parties, and meetings have been held with the Board of Directors and the Accounts Department.

There are many advantages to this system. The office is operating for a longer period of time, and this extension of business hours would benefit the company's overseas clients whose time zones are different from those of the UK. We would also be able to offer a service for clients at weekends. Staggered hours would relieve pressure on office equipment and managers' time, and would create a more spacious environment. Staff well-being is further increased by avoidance of the rush-hour, and more effective use of days off, thus boosting staff morale and efficiency. Employees will be able to choose a day off mid-week in lieu of Saturday, a choice which may lead to an improvement in their leisure time and, in turn, have a positive effect on their working performance.

The cost of such a scheme is considerable; overheads will increase by an estimated 7%, although this may be offset by other benefits, such as reduced insurance premiums and photocopying costs, not to mention a substantial increase in productivity.

The conclusion we reached after careful analysis of the information provided in the questionnaires, departmental reports, and the 'Costing Sheet Estimate', is that the introduction of a flexitime system would be viable financially, and popular with the majority of staff. We therefore recommend its introduction within the next six months.

16 Personnel appointments

16.a

1 c	6 d	11 d
2 a	7 d	12 d
3 c	8 a	13 b
4 c	9 d	14 b
5 d	10 d	15 b

16.b

1 Most of our computers are manufactured in Korea.
2 If there hadn't been a strike, we would have sent the consignment by rail.
3 He asked me if I knew what the dollar rate was.
4 He apologized for not replying sooner.
5 By the time you arrive, the Manager will have left.
6 I am interested in these latest sales forecasts.
7 I have been working with NCR for three weeks.
8 My secretary types very efficiently.
9 The representative wanted to know when the sales conference finished.
10 If I had the right qualifications, I would apply for a transfer.

16.c

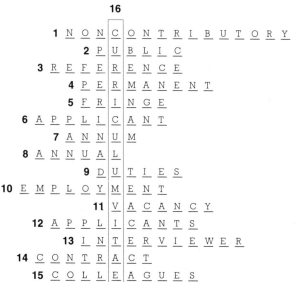

```
16
 1 N O N C O N T R I B U T O R Y
       2 P U B L I C
   3 R E F E R E N C E
       4 P E R M A N E N T
         5 F R I N G E
 6 A P P L I C A N T
       7 A N N U M
 8 A N N U A L
         9 D U T I E S
10 E M P L O Y M E N T
        11 V A C A N C Y
     12 A P P L I C A N T S
       13 I N T E R V I E W E R
   14 C O N T R A C T
     15 C O L L E A G U E S
```

16.d

1	fluent	6 acting
2	applicant	7 duties
3	experience	8 application form
4	advantage	9 reference
5	includes	

16.e Model letter:

Sender: Carla Giuliani, 114 Ellesmere Walk, Finchley, London NW3 1DP
Date: 23 May 19—
Receiver: The Personnel Manager, International Publishing Ltd., 60 Girton Street,
Cambridge CB2 3EU

Dear Ms Prentiss

Bilingual Secretary Ref. PP391

Please find enclosed my completed application form.

As you will see, I can speak a number of European languages, as well as having the necessary academic and secretarial qualifications which I think would be useful to your organization. I feel I would respond well to such a challenging post.

I would also welcome the opportunity to learn as much as I can about the publishing profession.

I hope to have the chance to discuss the post in more detail at an interview. If, meanwhile, you require any further information, please contact me.

I look forward to hearing from you.

Yours sincerely

Carla Giuliani

Enc.

16.f Model letter:

Sender: International Publishing Ltd., 60 Girton Street, Cambridge CB2 3EU
Date: 2 June 19—
Receiver: Carla Giuliani, 114 Ellesmere Walk, Finchley, London NW3 1DP

Dear Miss Giuliani

I am writing to you, on behalf of the Managing Director, to ask you if you could come to our offices on 18 June at 14.30. Prior to the interview with him, there will be an Italian and French translation test.

I have enclosed a map showing you how to get here; there are frequent trains from Liverpool Street Station.

Please telephone me on Extn. 412 to confirm that you will be able to attend, or to arrange another time if this is not convenient.

I look forward to meeting you.

Yours sincerely

Paula Prentiss
Personnel Manager
Enc.

16.g   Model letter:

Sender: International Publishing Ltd., 60 Girton Street, Cambridge CB2 3EU
Date: 22 June 19—
Receiver: Carla Giuliani, 114 Ellesmere Walk, Finchley, London NW3 1DP

Dear Miss Giuliani

Bilingual Secretary PP391

I am pleased to inform you that you have been accepted for the above post, for which you were interviewed on 18 June.

Your duties are to commence on 3 August 19—, and you will be responsible to Mr Mark Dowland, Assistant Manager.

Enclosed are two copies of the contract of employment. Please sign one copy and return it to Paula Prentiss as soon as possible.

I am sure you will be happy working here, and we look forward to seeing you at 09.00 on 3 August.

Yours sincerely

Kevin Wheeler
Managing Director

Enc.